BY *Morrie A. Moss*

# THE IMPORTANCE OF UNIMPORTANCE

SHELBY HOUSE

1989

Shelby House
1407 Union Avenue
401 Mid-Memphis Tower
Memphis, Tennessee 38104

Copyright ©1989 by Morrie A. Moss

ISBN-0-942-179-08-0: $14.95

Cover Design by Larry Pardue
Typography by Patterson Publications, Inc.

All rights reserved. No part of this book may be used or reproduced in any manner whatsoever without written permission except in the case of brief quotations embodied in critical articles and reviews. For information address Shelby House, 1407 Union Avenue, 401 Mid-Memphis Tower, Memphis, Tennessee 38104

## DEDICATION

To all the people who are living or who have ever lived on this earth. Each, in his own special way, has contributed something to mankind.

## PURPOSE

As I enter my 80th year, I find myself becoming more philosophical. Writing these short essays on subjects which I have been thinking about has given me the pleasure of putting my thoughts on paper. I will be pleased if the essays can stimulate your thinking, whether in agreement or disagreement! I am neither a preacher nor a teacher but a businessman. Perhaps this makes the essays more unique.

# CONTENTS

| | | |
|---|---|---|
| One | *Giving* | 13 |
| Two | *Envy* | 19 |
| Three | *Philandering* | 21 |
| Four | *The Best I Can* | 23 |
| Five | *Why?* | 25 |
| Six | *Luck* | 27 |
| Seven | *Gray Skies* | 29 |
| Eight | *Enough* | 33 |
| Nine | *Repetition* | 37 |
| Ten | *Equal* | 39 |
| Eleven | *Art* | 41 |
| Twelve | *Mausoleum* | 45 |
| Thirteen | *Odds* | 47 |
| Fourteen | *Leadership* | 49 |
| Fifteen | *Exit* | 53 |
| Sixteen | *Water* | 57 |
| Seventeen | *Speech* | 59 |
| Eighteen | *Molding* | 61 |
| Nineteen | *Leaves* | 65 |
| Twenty | *Super Bowl* | 67 |
| Twenty-one | *Lonely* | 69 |
| Twenty-two | *You* | 71 |
| Twenty-three | *"?"* | 73 |
| Twenty-four | *Prejudice* | 79 |
| Twenty-five | *May 1* | 81 |

| | | |
|---:|:---|---:|
| Twenty-six | *Mirror* | 85 |
| Twenty-seven | *Sad* | 69 |
| Twenty-eight | *Nuttin'* | 89 |
| Twenty-nine | *Special* | 91 |
| Thirty | *Choice* | 93 |
| Thirty-one | *Expectations* | 95 |
| Thirty-two | *Heroes* | 97 |
| Thirty-three | *Attrition* | 99 |
| Thirty-four | *Death* | 101 |
| Thirty-five | *Amazing!* | 103 |
| Thirty-six | *Appreciation* | 105 |
| Thirty-seven | *Beauty* | 107 |
| Thirty-eight | *Color* | 109 |
| Thirty-nine | *Dissent* | 111 |
| Forty | *Sorry* | 113 |
| Forty-one | *Landmarks* | 117 |
| Forty-two | *Turmoil* | 119 |
| Forty-three | *Prestigious* | 121 |
| Forty-four | *The Importance of Unimportance!* | 123 |

# 1

# GIVING

I assume nothing just happens. A response come from a stimulus. What motivates a person to give monetary gifts? Gifts of love, sacrifice or service may or may not have a greater value than gifts of money, but here I am considering only the reasons for monetary gifts. I find there are three types of giving:

## The Gift for Personal Gain

When a philanthropic person makes a substantial gift to a school, hospital, community or church, what motivated this benevolence? Was it a gift of appreciated property to get a maximum tax deduction? During the second World War, a wealthy friend of mine in the wholesale liquor business was making more money than he ever had. Grain alcohol had been rationed for the war effort and was permitted only for medicinal purposes. It required a doctor's prescription and was dispensed through drug stores. Therefore, any alcoholic beverages on the market brought high prices. Before rationing began, this friend had amassed a tremendous inventory of bottled alcoholic drinks. He parceled out his inventory very sparingly but, nevertheless, in those days of up to a 94% income tax, he would reach that bracket in the first month of the year. In addition to his stock of bottled liquor, he had purchased whiskey in bulk for a good many years prior to rationing. He had paid about 40 cents a gallon and now could get about $15 a gallon.

This man had never been particularly charity-minded but, after it was called to his attention that he could make more of a profit by giving this whiskey away, he was transformed into a liberal contributor.

The financial windfall that motivated his sudden conversion to generosity worked out this way: Because the warehouse receipts for bulk whiskey were a part of his business, it was subject to ordinary income tax provisions. If he sold it, his profit would have been $14.60 a gallon and his tax would be $13.72, leaving him a net return of $1.28 per gallon. If he gave it away, he could deduct $15 from his gross income, giving him 94%—or $14.10 instead of $1.28 per gallon. If he had been in California he would have saved even more because the California tax on top of the federal tax would have exceeded 100%. The tax laws as to allowable deductions and tax rates have changed since then, but the moral remains: it can be financially rewarding to be a philanthropist.

That philanthropist-for-profit had two sisters of moderate means. I suggested that he give each of his sisters 5% of his business, which would only cost him 6% of his income. They, in turn, being in low income tax brackets, could keep much more. This additional income could brighten their lives by allowing them to buy desirable things that they otherwise could not afford. He hesitated, but finally consented to this plan, and the first year brought each of his sisters about $25,000 after taxes. When he learned the size of their income, he immediately revoked his gifts. I asked him why, and he replied that he didn't want to make fools of people. My conclusion was that he had determined the only person capable of handling or having money was himself.

Another source of selfish giving is the frequent case of pressure giving or, in fact, extortion. A customer will ask a businessman for a gift to some charity in which the customer has a particular interest, but the businessman has none. How should he respond? If he gives, it is because of pressure. If he doesn't give, he fears business reprisals. Rationalizing, he gives, figuring it is cheaper to give money than lose a customer. He, too, is a philanthropist and is lauded for his generosity and kind heart.

These so-called charitable contributions that are motivated by a monetary gain comprise a large segment of monetary gifts.

## The Gift of Self-Indulgence

What is the motivation of the individual who gives without

hopes of personal monetary gain? Certainly he gets a tax deduction for a charitable contribution, but despite the tax credit, a sizeable part of the gift is his own money. In effect, the amount of his contribution is partially shared by the government.

The newspapers today wrote about an 84-year-old man, an immigrant, who became extremely wealthy through his business acumen and hard work. He owned a chain of stores and reputedly had amassed a fortune of $750 million. However, the publicity came because of a $20,000 cash gift and a life annuity of $20,000 annually to a young girl model whose face had been severely mutilated in an attack by an assailant. Doctors advised her that the scarring would be permanent. The old man was so touched by her plight, a probably ruined modeling career, that he responded financially. No tax deduction was allowable. What was his motivation? Could it have been a desire for publicity? What do you think?

In 1950 I was touring Europe with my wife and two friends. We went to Assisi, home of St. Francis, and visited his church. It was a small building, very old, with small cubicles in which small statues of saints stood and where gifts could be deposited. I noticed a very tiny coin, about the size of a pea, amongst the contributions and inquired as to its value. Our guide informed us this was 1/10 lira. Post-war inflation had made the dollar worth 767 liras. Just imagine 767 liras to one dollar and 1/10 of a lira! The thought of the widow's mite comes to mind, and I speculated this must have been a very poor person who made this gift. What was the motivation? Could it have been hopes of a boost towards heaven? What do you think?

Rather frequently (although probably not frequent enough) we read of gifts to schools, museums, hospitals and churches. Some large gifts are probably motivated by ego—a building named after you or a special program named for you. Many philanthropists are encouraged to make gifts by being rewarded with perpetual recognition. Is that the motivation for their giving?

On the other hand, many generous people prefer anonymity. They give but require no public announcement of their gifts. What is their motivation? Could it be a fear that publicity would cause a deluge of requests for similar gifts for other causes?

Then we have the individual who, with no apparent motivation, gives liberally to a charity. This person is not concerned with publicity and does not covet special recognition. In fact, he may contribute to many unrelated causes. What motivates this person? Could it be just the personal satisfaction? Could it fill a desire to contribute to causes? In many ways, this is a very fortunate person. He is able to get pleasure out of giving, with the personal pleasure being his sole reward. How sad that so many donors have never experienced the spiritual uplift, the great joy of being able to give.

## The Gift of Guilt and Fear

The labor union movement has neglected one segment of our society, namely, the domestic worker. In the South particularly, exploitation of domestics has been the practice. I am sure it exists all over the country, but I note what I am most familiar with. Domestics have been demeaned by a paternalistic concept of their inability to properly handle money, a justifiable assumption in many cases. They are paid as little as possible in many cases, with the justification that their employers will take care of them. They are deprived of pensions, bonuses, vacations and most of the amenities considered a prerogative of labor. Instead, they are dependent upon the largess of the boss. When we realize the comfort and pleasure provided by domestics, it is hard to justify the employers' lack of financial appreciation. I note, although in all too few instances, some wills provide for domestics. What is this motivation? Could it be guilt?

Another carrot dangled before particularly desirable domestics is the bonus or pay-raise at intervals, depending upon their continuing employment. Would this come under the title of incentive, or perhaps would it indicate bondage?

People have always given freely to a deity whether it be an idol, many gods, one god or just a belief in an unknown power. These gifts of sacrifices, money or other items of value are given in hope of a reward of some kind. Some people with guilt complexes try to buy relief by donating a building or money to a religion. What is the motivation? Is it to eradicate the guilt, by divine intervention, because of the gift? Is it to buy a passport to eternal happiness?

I have found gamblers and underworld characters exceptionally generous, particularly to religious causes. Since these people are engaged in illegal activities, their contributions are generally in cash and anonymous. This might be a prime example of giving because of guilt. Some gamblers are also generous because they are subject to pressure or outright extortion from a law enforcement agency. I lived in Chicago and Miami during periods of mob control. Capone's gang and the Meyer Lansky syndicate contributed generously to charity. Was guilt their motivation?

## Wrapping It Up

I believe all monetary gifts can be put in one of those three categories: giving for monetary gain, giving for ego or giving because of guilt or fear. How would you classify some other instances: The hand from the grave trying to control gifts made after death by attempting to attach permanent strings. The law took care of that by limiting the attempt at perpetuity to only twenty-one years. Was the giver motivated by fear and insecurity?

Perhaps the greatest gift of all is not a gift, but a loan. To assist a person in reaching his goal of an education, a career or a business can bring great personal joy and pride to the donor. To be able to help without demeaning the recipient, by not giving but lending without expecting a reward, is noble. That nobility can be enhanced by later specifying that the loan is not to be repaid, but instead is to start a cycle of meaningful giving by affording another the chance you have had.

Assuming that all monetary gifts are for a good purpose, I conclude that the results are the same regardless of the motivation.

# 2

# ENVY

Haven't we all envied something we didn't have but somebody else did have? I envy him... I wish I had his energy... I wish I had his youth... I wish I had his money... I wish I had his looks... I wish I had his education... I wish I had his brains... I wish, I wish and I wish! Why do we envy others? Why can't we adjust to what we have or, not resigning ourselves to our fate, constantly strive to attain the something that we want? Instead of wishing, why can't we do?

Unless we have a very narrow vision and goal, I do not believe it possible ever to attain all the things we would like to have or to do. Life is constant change. Present desires may be the futures's follies. However, envying will not attain the objects of envy.

I knew a man who was quite wealthy, but always envious of others. He had more than enough worldly goods to take care of himself and his family in handsome fashion. Yet, instead of counting his blessings, he kept envying those who perhaps had more of the worldly goods that he didn't need. In fact, this envy nagged so much that the man sold his business, moved away from the city that had created his fortune and hibernated in Miami, Florida. He did not want to see others prosper. His old friends who would come to Florida for the winters sometimes went to the horse races for entertainment. He went every day, dressed shabbily and unshaven, and spent his time with the track hands whose poverty and misfortune would not make him envious. He hid from his friends for fear of hearing good news from them. I like to think of this unfortunate person as one who would be delighted to hear that a friend lost a bet with another friend. He would laugh like a hyena until he realized that the other friend had won the bet. That would distress him. Perhaps if the winner would have had a stroke at the point of winning, then the man would be satisfied. This type of envy or jealousy comes from an extremely neurotic individual.

An unfortunate type of envy causes resentment and is begrudging. Some friends with their teenage daughter were visiting another more affluent person who happened to have a big beautiful home. The girl asked her dad why they didn't have a home like that. He replied, "That's a good question." His resentment toward its owner was apparent.

Perhaps admiration would be a good alternative to envy. To admire instead of envy would create a more positive attitude and perhaps the stimulus to emulate. Admiration in itself will not accomplish the desire for attainment, but it can be the motivation toward that goal.

## Envy

He's old but rich.
I'm young and poor.
I wish I were him.
He travels. I don't.
He doesn't work. I do.
I wish I were him.
He has a big home and cars.
I don't! I wish I were him.
He knows prominent people.
He goes to many gala functions.
I don't! I wish I were him.
He's young and eager.
I've been young and eager.
I wish I were him.
He will see much of the future.
I have seen much of the past.
I wish I were him.

# 3
# PHILANDERING

We all have been preached to about the virtuous life. The Ten Commandments forbid adultery and also lust in coveting another's wife. Yet, in spite of all the moralistic reasons not to be a philanderer, I would like to approach the subject from a selfish standpoint—why abstinence is more desirable than succumbing to the temptations of philandering.

Even a former President of the United States has confessed to lust. That, in itself, would not glorify the feeling but, tritely, let's say all of us are human, and perhaps lust exists in us all.

Why shouldn't we gratify the lust that we feel? There are three great obstacles: guilt, fear of detection and limited pleasure.

Guilt can be devastating! The constant nagging of yourself, the loss of self-respect and the remorse can become unbearable. Why create guilt that will last forever for a few moments of stolen pleasure? It is easy to create guilt but difficult to cope with it and more difficult, if not impossible, to eradicate it.

In carrying on an illicit affair, you are constantly sneaking, hiding, concealing and lying. The fear of getting caught keeps you constantly in an unhealthy state of nervous tension. Why create an avoidable unpleasant situation?

Why should anyone wish to settle for less pleasure than is available? Why should you accept half an apple when you want and can have the whole apple? When you divide your sexual activities among more than one person, you are depriving yourself and partner of the maximum thrill that is possible to attain. It is reasonable and true that dividing your sexual activities results in a division of your intensity.

Thus I can conclude that for purely selfish reasons, it is not wise to philander.

# 4

# THE BEST I CAN

I'm doing the best I can! How often have we heard that. Maybe we, too, have said it. How do we know we are doing the best we can? What is doing the best we can? What if the best we can is not enough?

When we are told to do something new, for which we have no training or skill, we try to do it and sometimes we fail, because we were not qualified to do the job. We tried our best, but to no avail. If it is important to do the assigned task, then we must learn to do it. If a job depends upon it and we still can't do it, quite obviously we must get another job. Will the fact that we failed be devastating? Can we rationalize that we did the best we could? Can we be happy with the conclusion? Can we at least take comfort in the knowledge that we tried? Can perseverance, desire and effort assuage the "agony of defeat"?

Successful completion of the assigned task doesn't necessarily mean that we have done the best we can. If I am chairman of a fund drive to raise a specific sum and I do it, would this be the best I can? What if I could have raised more but settled for the goal assigned? Or if I am a student in college and am in the top 10%. I'm on the Dean's list. I think I'm doing the best I can ... but am I? How about being No. 1 and even then trying to do better? Is there any way to measure my nearness to the best I can do? I think not. If we reach for the stars, even though we know we will never reach them, we will know we are doing the best we can. That is better than reaching for a dandelion which, in effect, may not be reaching at all. How do we know we are doing the best we can? This is difficult to answer. I would guess if we continued trying for excellence and kept making progress until we reached an impasse, we might know that we had done the best we could. Then again, the impasse might indicate only that our ability needs to be enhanced by further learning, experience or trial and error effort. If we continued to progress after supplemental training, it would illustrate that we had not done the best we could.

I knew a wonderful lady stricken by an incurable disease. Slowly but surely she began deteriorating. The first year brought shaky walking; the second year inability to walk; the third year inability to sit; the fourth, fifth and sixth years complete immobility, inability to speak, to move or do anything without assistance. During this ordeal, I remember her determined effort and her plaintive cry of discouragement, "I am trying so hard." Even during the last three years, her effort continued. Her lips would move but no sound came out. Her desire to get well and her courage continued, but without success. I feel certain she was doing the best she could—the best anybody could do in similar circumstances. I am convinced of this even to the end, when my wife died.

# 5
# WHY?

Much of the progress in society is triggered by the inquiring mind. Why is this? The constant desire for reasons can and does prohibit complacency. Seemingly unanswerable "whys" create problems for acceptance. The dilemma is that with an inquiring mind attempting to find logical answers, you are constantly groping and are never at peace; you fail to accept the comfort that is possible through acceptance.

You have heard, "The Bible says it. I believe it. That settles it." How wonderful to obtain complete relief from nagging doubts by accepting unanswerable questions. Why does the Bible say it? Why do I believe it? Why does that settle it?

It is certainly more convenient and comfortable to accept majority opinions. The world is flat. It isn't, but this fact was only found by nonconformance. An inquiring mind asked why did the apple fall down instead of up, and the law of gravity was discovered.

In religion, an inquiring mind is particularly troublesome because some questions are unanswerable. Many different religions and their various denominations exist because of different outcomes of attempting to reach the same objective with varied philosophical approaches. Inquiry cannot find answers to everything, yet without it we have no progress. On the other hand, some can gain great comfort through not understanding but accepting.

He is dead. We mourn. We accept. We adjust. We rationalize. All the whys in the world will not bring him back. We comfort ourselves by accepting this as the will of God. Many of us do not attempt to ask why did he die. Some ask, "Why him? Why not me?" Logic will not explain the unsolvable and inevitable death, yet inquiry will be beneficial. Medical experts can learn from science, and friends can learn by inspiration or by avoidance of whatever indiscretions the deceased may have committed—so, even in death, the constant search continues for reasons why.

Recently a newspaper article reported that the Soviet policy of teaching atheism in schools has had an unintentional effect. It has made young people curious enough about religion to come to church. This is truly remarkable in a totalitarian society where the state tells people how and what to think. Here we have people asking why.

## Conclusion

People can be classified in three groups by their attitude to the inquiring mind that asks "why." The first is the happy group who unreservedly accept what they are taught, told or ordered. "Ours not to reason why, ours but to do and die." They have no doubts and no questions. They attain complacency and peace of mind by believing what other people have determined is right and wrong.

Another group are probers who constantly ask why, are never completely satisfied, and are never sure they have discovered the answer. They are constantly digging and searching for answers.

The third group accepts but also can still ask why. They eliminate potentially difficult questions by accepting that those are beyond their capacity to tackle.

Which is preferable? It's such a complicated puzzle to me that I'm wondering WHY I wrote it.

# 6

# LUCK

Napoleon was looking for a new field marshal and called in a young general for an interview. In response to Napoleon's questions the young general told of his abilities. His life had been devoted to the military. He was intensely loyal to the emperor Napoleon and devoutly loved France. He had been educated in one of the finest military schools in Europe and had been a brilliant scholar. He had served his country and emperor in many battles with great distinction. His loyalty, patriotism, abilities and valor were unquestionable. However, with all this glowing evidence, which Napoleon admired and appreciated, one important question remained to be answered. "General, are you lucky?"

Lady Luck, please smile on me! It's better to be lucky than smart. But you make your own luck. Being prepared and taking advantage of an opportunity avoids the necessity for luck. Webster defines luck as success by chance rather than merit. The definition goes further to include being fortunate, which he says is suggestive of a favorable accident and a hint of being watched over by a higher power or being blessed beyond one's desires. Another definition of lucky would imply help or intervention of providence.

The strict interpretation of lucky as success by chance instead of merit may not always be correct. Let's take the case of two brilliant friends. In school they earned equal distinction. Both graduated from the same prestigious law college. Both were much sought after and hired by different prominent law firms. One became famous, wealthy and more important than his equally competent friend because of exposure to more sensational and publicized law suits. The other performed brilliantly and successfully in almost total anonymity. Why? Luck? As far as merit, both had ample. Yet by chance one got into the limelight and the other didn't. We might ask, so what? Maybe both are happy with their lives. Maybe the less prominent lawyer is happy without the stress and obligations of fame. Maybe the famous one envies his friend. Then again, maybe not.

The element of providence appears in all facets of luck. We cannot explain the work of providence.

The search for elusive luck can be devastating. The compulsive gambler is a born loser waiting for his luck to change while, in the meantime, he loses self-respect, endangers the welfare of his family and, in some cases, even resorts to theft in the insatiable quest for the lucky strike.

Does God smile on some of his people and ignore others? Does God dole out success, money, fame and happiness to his favorites? I think not. Inspiration certainly can be obtained by a spiritual faith that may help attain success. Yet this is available to anyone who cares to seek it. Maybe the old saying "God helps them that help themselves" is true. How do you get to be a Prince? Strictly by chance without merit. How do you get to be President of the United States? Out of 200 million people, one is chosen. Why? Is he most capable, the most knowledgeable, the best man for the job? Probably not. Undoubtedly there are many others of equal, if not greater, abilities. Wouldn't you say luck is all-important in all those instances? And so it goes, in example after example, some fortuitous event fashioning life.

# 7

# GRAY SKIES

This morning, riding to work on a humid, warm, cloudy day, I noticed a small patch of blue sky with the sun brightly shining through. It indeed was a contrast to the dull, ominous gray and black clouds completely covering the sky with the exception of this one blue spot. I got to thinking, isn't this typical of life? Don't we experience moods of gray skies? Isn't it true that the mood changes? Nothing really remains permanent in a life. Isn't it also true that behind the murky clouds of gray, blue skies exist?

The presence of unseen blue skies can lead to a complacency, motivated by belief that the clouds are just a temporary sorrow in life soon to be assuaged by the blue skies. Is this true? Surely it is comforting to rest in the assurance that the depression will only be temporary. Is this realistic?

Are there lives where blue skies never appear? Is it inevitable that sunshine follows the rain? What about an incurable disease creating constant pain? What about the unfortunate who never can find a place in life either economically or socially? Is there a remedy?

I believe there is! We do not have to accept gray skies. We can look forward to their passing and the return of blue. However, if we have no reason to expect this, what should we do? We should adjust our lives to accept our fate—not to relish, enjoy or be happy with it. Some of the gray skies that we are to be burdened with for life cannot evaporate or be wished away. We must accept them when there is no alternative. But acceptance does not mean resignation. In a life of gray skies, perhaps this passive acceptance will allow us small pieces of the blue, and perhaps we can pattern our behavior to detect some blue in the gray.

I knew a remarkable blind man. He was jeweler and became incurably blind through a blow on his head in a cricket game. He had enjoyed sight most of his life but his middle age and beyond were to be lived in blindness. I hesitate to use darkness. He was fortunate to have a family who could help in his jewelry shop. However, the spark, the motivation, the personality of the business was the handicapped man. After a few minutes talking with him, you forgot he was blind. This was what he wanted. He would look you in the eye and talk cheerfully with an ingratiating smile. I'm certain that he had many spells of depression, but kept them well shielded from his friends and customers. His gray skies remained inside. He emanated the sun and the blue skies. He was ambitious, industrious and productive. He tried to live a normal life. He headed, effectively, blind organizations. I remember in particular a gala black tie affair in a luxury hotel to raise funds for "Fight for Sight." The crowd was large and there was considerable grumbling as to seat assignments. This man rose to the occasion. He silenced all complaints completely by saying, "If you have your eyesight, you have the best seat in the house."

A distinguished professor at a major university, an author, poet and teacher, lived in gray skies all of his life. At the age of four, his nurse took him to a railroad station to meet some arriving passengers. He wandered from his nurse to the railroad track where he became petrified and terrified by a steam engine, whistle blasting, smoke belching, moving toward him. His nurse rescued him from physical damage, but a horrible neurotic condition stayed with him for life. He could never be alone. The desolate feeling of helplessness and fear at being all alone on the railroad track left an indelible blot on his mind. Only the scientific explanation of his condition conveyed by psychiatrists kept him from insanity and probable suicide. This brilliant and otherwise normal man had to be in the presence of someone at all times. All his life, his wife, companions or friends always were with him. Out of these gray clouds, inspired teaching, sensitive poetry and fiction emanated. This was the blue sky of his life.

In Memphis many years ago, an annual football game was played to provide funds for the blind. Each halftime, the lights were turned off symbolizing the eternal gray skies of darkness suffered by the blind. Matches were then lit, illuminating the stadium with an eerie glow. This symbolized the light to be brought into the lives of the blind. The warmth from the matches was to symbolize love and compassion for all people. This was the blue sky.

"Into each life, some rain must fall." It can be a few drops, a shower, a cloudburst or a hurricane. It can last a moment, an hour, a day, a year or forever. Into each life, get as many blue skies as you can. My blue skies are a smile, a note or a letter saying "Thank you!" What are yours?

# 8

# ENOUGH

The other night a friend said to me, "I have enough money. I don't want any more." This was not a new expression to me. Haven't we all heard, "We have everything we want . . . We have all we need . . . I've done enough in life for others so from now on out I'll do it for myself . . . I've given the kids an education and that's enough—it's more than I got." Probably you can fill in some other enoughs.

What is enough? What do we have enough of? Some people never have enough wealth. Is that good or bad? Some people never have enough time. Some people never get enough rest, recreation or pleasure. Some people seem always happy. Some people seem always sad.

Greed, desire for power, plus insecurity are the motivations for the person who never has enough money. The more he has, the more he wants. It becomes a challenge, a neurotic reaction to keep grasping to get more. Money to him represents power and, in a sense, he is entirely correct. Money has great persuasive powers. Money opens doors to social climbers, even though this is not enough for certain ethnic groups to invade the inner sanctum of bigots. Yet, it commands a reluctant approbation and even envy among many.

Irrespective of motivation, what is the good of amassing a fortune beyond your personal capacity to use it? Because it is impossible to satisfy the insatiable greed of people, continual accumulation of wealth produces only a hoard and, in most instances, has no purpose. Moralizing a bit, I would suggest that the constant, determined quest of limitless wealth can be very worthwhile if, instead of being hoarded, the money is distributed for good causes. The huge fortunes are, as a rule, used this way. Most modest fortunes are not.

On the other hand, suppose the person thinks he has enough wealth for his family and self and chooses to retire. What are the possibilities in this case? Firstly, it's rather selfish to sacrifice the talents that enabled him to do what he has done and, secondly, there are negative possibilities of abandoning a productive life for retirement. These may be boredom, a loss of contact with old associates, creation of imaginary ills, etc. It is almost criminal for useful, talented individuals such as doctors, lawyers, musicians, teachers and clergymen to say, "Enough, no more, I've had it!" Age has limitations. Accept these, but don't abandon what is still possible to do and create a premature death. Paradoxically, many people who want to continue have been forced to retire by age limitations. Recognizing the unfairness of forced retirement for competent people, a strong movement is underway to eliminate compulsory retirement.

Perfection is impossible to attain, but the continued effort to approach perfection can be the powerful motivation in life. Who has ever had all the knowledge there is? Who has ever done all the good there is to be done? Who has ever been able to solve all the mysteries, the puzzles of life? So many great and vital parts of our existence need more and never have reached enough. Medicine—as progressive, innovative and advanced as it has become—is still nowhere near the solution of major discoveries. How do you cure cancer? What causes cancer? How can life be prolonged indefinitely? Religion in some form is practiced universally. When and how can all people accept a universal religion? The poor are always with us. How can we eradicate poverty, ignorance and intolerance? Opportunities are always available to some. How can we make them available to all?

There is so much to be done and so little time to do it, that to say, "Enough!" may not only be selfish but very insensitive to those who do not have enough. Doesn't there come a time in every life when it might be justifiable to say, "I did all I could. Now I want to spend the rest of my days doing nothing or what I want to do." Maybe. Yet if every successful person felt this way, what would happen to solve the existing problems?

Slowing down may be advisable or necessary. It is also true that a fanatic, solitary aim of trying to solve all of the existing problems could react negatively into a counter-productive effort.

As long as problems remain to be solved and as long as people are able to contribute efforts, no matter how small, and ideas to help solve them, we have never had or done enough.

# 9

## REPETITION

How are things going? How are you today? Have a good day! How do you feel? So glad to see you! What's new?

I'm sure you have heard those many times. They supposedly indicate an interest in a person, but constant repetition reduces them to a robot-like automation that is devoid of personal interest, boring and in many cases irritating.

A response given by an acquaintance to "How do you feel?" was "Do you really care?" I used to think that very rude and insensitive and would reply in kind by "I really don't give a damn!" (Rhett Butler, please excuse the plagiarism.) However, I realize that the question "How do you feel?" was really not a sincere question but a supposed effort at propriety. It seems like an inquisitor feigning interest in something which in fact he has no interest.

Why always questions? Wouldn't good morning, good evening, hello or goodbye be easier, more proper and not requiring an explanation? Usually the automatic similarly robotic response to "How are you?" is "Fine. How are you?" If a simple hello and goodbye are inadequate, what about a positive "You surely look great!"

I have on occasion run into the same person three times in one day—a morning meeting of some sort, a casual passing at lunch time and another evening meeting. Admittedly this was rare, but the "So glad to see you!" each time we met three times in one day almost prompted me to say, "Since you derive so much pleasure out of seeing me, I'm going to send you my picture and then you can look at it and be glad whenever you please."

This is not an attempt to be critical of accepted conduct of society. Certainly it is better to acknowledge a person with some form of recognition rather than none at all. Can't a little sincerity, a little variety be blended into the exercise?

# 10

# EQUAL

"All men are created equal." Is this true? Maybe most people will be physically equal—that is, have two arms, two legs, a head, eyes and ears. Some will not have all these things. Most will have a normal brain. Some will not. The many diseases passed on to children will certainly not be the same in all. The many other variations that exist suggest that all men are not created equal.

Among other things not equal, we would find color—white, yellow, red, black and mixed. Each color has advantages and disadvantages, but they certainly are not equal.

Accidents of birth create inequalities... born to nobility, born to wealth, born to drunkards, dope addicts, criminals, born to the clergy, the arts, the professions or business world.

Thus all children are not born equal. Yet, that is just the beginning. Does this mean we must go through life unequal? Certainly not! The closest we can come to equality is affording the opportunity to reach equality. In a free society such as the United States, it is believed by some that all have the same opportunities. This is not true. Prejudices and customs make it impossible to achieve absolute equality among many people. It may be possible to achieve equality in a small group of peers.

Nevertheless, who do you want to be equal with? What kind of equality do you aspire to—wealth or knowledge? These you have the opportunity to attain.

Let's assume a Utopian situation where all men are equal in every way—physically, mentally and morally. Let's also assume they start life from scratch equal in every respect. How long do you think this equality would last?

# 11

## ART

Museum art is supposed to represent a cultural peak and is considered a requisite for good living in cities or towns capable of supporting a museum. Because museums are supposed to be essential to the cultural climate of a community, practically all cities have facilities to further the arts. However, most museums have very limited attendance and meager financial support. Why is this?

Most communities with large European ethnic populations patronize and support the museums because the people have been indoctrinated with the art culture from childhood. Any European city of importance will have its museum or museums. A constant stream of school children visit these museums, getting an exposure to art at an impressionable age that will remain with them through life.

The populations of many cities in the United States are so far removed from their ethnic origin that the arts are forgotten. In other words, the job of making a living, supporting and raising a family, has, in many cases, removed the desire to enjoy the arts. The elitist association of art is a turn-off to most. "Why should I go to a museum? It's not for me. It's for society people. I know nothing about art. I'd feel out of place looking at things I don't understand. Why should I support museums that I have no interest in?" All are valid questions and conclusions. If we accept the concept that art is a necessity of a cultured society, then we have the task and duty to spread the message, "Art is for everyone."

Adults who have never enjoyed art are reluctant to become exposed to it. We all have our likes and dislikes. We go to church social events, play golf, watch baseball and football, go to parks, swim, walk. We have a full active life, but have we? I am not advocating giving up or radically changing anybody's mode of living; however, it seems to me that exposing oneself to the arts for a tiny bit of time, no matter how small the bit, could be helpful spiritually and emotionally. A casual quick visit to a museum could develop a liking and appreciation of some form of art. You go as far as you desire, maybe come back, maybe become interested in a painting because of its subject or color, a sculpture, a porcelain, a tapestry, a rug, a piece of silver or glass, a textile, a photograph. You have many things to choose from. At least give yourself an opportunity to participate in a museum which you are supporting directly through your taxes.

How do we get across the idea that art is for everyone and not merely the right of a privileged few? As just said, everyone is supporting, in a limited financial way, museums owned by the city, county, state or country. You are not getting your money's worth unless you use the museum.

However, the indoctrination, love and appreciation of art must begin with the children. This is being recognized and is being acted upon by our schools. Public schools are more and more offering instructions in art, both in appreciation, participation and history. Museums are building rooms especially for children to become involved in artistic creativity. We are all familiar with school windows and rooms decorated with pumpkins, witches and goblins for Halloween or with decorations for other holidays—Christmas, July 4th or Thanksgiving. Children are the focus of the program "Art is for Everyone." Many of them become lovers, patrons and benefactors of the arts when they grow up, and a domino syndrome is created where they will teach their children and on and on. In addition, the parents, interested in what their children are doing, get a taste of art that may create interest and support.

The elitist concept is also being diluted as more and more diversified groups are brought into active participation as trustees or docents. The museum facilities are even used for group meetings. It is gratifying to view the diversified crowds that now come to museum show openings. What used to be a black tie society event now has become a genuinely public affair at which people of all colors, ages, religions, social and financial status, in casual and semi-formal dress, mingle together. Of course, there are special events rewarding major supporters of the museum, but these are usually ceremonies prior to the official openings of new exhibitions.

Art education is being dispensed not only through museums and schools but also through television and public lectures.

If museum art, music, drama and the other arts, are a necessary part of a cultured community, then they should get the support of the people, both financially and by active participation in art. Appreciation, love and support of the arts comes through knowledge, which is being sponsored through the schools, through the media and through the government.

# 12

## MAUSOLEUM

The funeral service was over. We were told to leave because it would be about two hours before the body would be interred in its mausoleum crypt. I had been in the mausoleum before, but now it was somewhat startling to see my name on top of her name on the crypt she had purchased but which I had never seen. Under her name, date of birth and death were written. I was pleased to see the dates had been omitted under my name. We had facetiously referred to the crypts as our condominium. I had preferred cremation, as other members of my immediate family had, but acquiesced to my wife's wishes.

No flowers were allowed in the mausoleum. The many floral offerings were displayed in the open air outside the entrance door. Every time I visit the mausoleum, I see the flowers from recent funerals, generally faded and dying. Nothing could be more impressive than the realization that the flowers which were in full bloom for the funerals have now withered and died exactly like the bodies in the mausoleum.

Like a magnet, I return to the mausoleum every Saturday morning. I sit for a few minutes and then leave. Sometimes my mind is not even on the reason for being there, and then I wonder why am I there? Certainly my wife no longer lies in the crypt, only a mass of bones. If we believe in the immortality of the soul, if we believe in a heaven as she did, or whatever we may believe about what happens after death, then we must accept the fact that what is in the crypt is only the shell of a corpse. The spirit, the soul, the life has departed . . . where to nobody knows.

So I think, why am I returning here every week to visit with something that isn't there? I can be comfortable with my wife's belief that she would be in heaven—wherever and whatever heaven is. I can be comfortable that she would be welcome with open arms, possessing all the qualifications necessary for admittance. I think, if she is in heaven, why am I here? I think, what is the reason for me being here? I look at the small space in which her bones are interred and think of "Free at last." Free of what—pain, sickness, loneliness, troubles, problems? Freedom would involve lack of confinement, and here in the crypt is absolute confinement. Yet, if only bones are there, what difference does it make, and why am I there?

I rationalize that this place is where her last mortal remains were interred; therefore, it has a meaning. Wouldn't the memories of over fifty years association be more meaningful? Wouldn't the bed she died in at home be more of a shrine? After all, she lived and died in the bed. She reached the crypt only after life.

Some things can't be explained. I guess this is one of them. Actually, I usually have no feelings of one kind or another upon leaving the mausoleum. It isn't like a visit to my wife. It isn't because I feel it obligatory. Has it become a habit? I don't know.

For the foreseeable future, I guess every Saturday morning will find me making my weekly visit.

Recently I saw in an Ann Landers column a poem attributed to an Indian prayer.

> Do not stand by my grave and weep
> I am not there, I do not sleep
> I am a thousand winds that blow
> I am a diamond glint on snow
> I am the sunlight on ripened grain
> I am the gentle autumn rain.

I ponder that poem. Maybe I have discovered the answer to my dilemma.

# 13

## ODDS

This subject is closely allied to the earlier topic, "Luck". But while luck presumes divine intervention, odds present an exact mathematical law of averages. In games of chance, such as cards or dice, the exact chances of any desired result can be computed mathematically by the laws of probability. Since cards and dice are inanimate objects, no variations are possible and the law of averages—over a period of time—will prevail.

Let's look at the biggest game of all, the game of life. No exact mathematical computation can determine your longevity. Yes, there is statistical data available from mortality tables showing life expectancy at various ages. Life insurance companies base their premiums on these tables. However, since no two people are alike, it is unrealistic to expect that an individual person's life will be exactly the same as the statistical average. The statistics for narrower categories of heredity, age, sex or health will give a more exact average, but still only an average. Since you are not dealing with inanimate objects, an exact formula is impossible.

There are tables showing statistics on students' probabilities of graduating from college. Averages are mathematically correct—so many leave school in the first year, so many in the second, etc. until out of the entrants to the recipients of a degree you can compute the average chances of graduation. However, so many variations exist that it would be erroneous to tell an entering student that his chances of getting a degree are a certain percentage. The schools' standards are different, the students' preparations are different, the students' motivation, family background and so many other factors enter into the computation that, once again, we must arrive at the conclusion that averages are correct but not applicable in the same degree at the individual level.

Let's look at success, whatever that may be. Many people believe money to be the measure of success. If so, averages exist showing how many millionaires there are, etc. However, once again, uniformity is not accurate due to the differences in individual ability, background, ambition and luck. All are important factors in money accumulation. Each individual must establish his own criteria for success. Does he want to be a teacher, a preacher, a doctor, a lawyer, a businessman or what? Does he want wealth, health, happiness, knowledge, skill in a profession? Statistics can be found for many of those criteria, but I doubt if statistics exist as to chances for happiness.

## CONCLUSION

The law of averages or odds will prevail over a period of time with inanimate objects. The law of averages or odds will also prevail over a period of time with animate objects. However, it will not apply the same to all individuals. Therefore, odds rather than by averages must be determined by individuals.

# 14

## LEADERSHIP

What are the qualities necessary for leadership?

### Inspiration

I believe the most important one is inspiration. The greatest leader of all would be God, who has inspired all of the religious leaders who, in turn, have inspired others. Yet the traditional concept of constant strife between good and evil reminds us that inspiration can be for good or evil. Some of the most inspiring individuals turned people into savages, as Hitler vividly demonstrated. On the other hand, people have been inspired to do great, good things in government, health, religion and education.

### Communication

In order to inspire people, you must be able to communicate. This can be accomplished calmly or emotionally. People can be whipped to a frenzy by inspirational communication. Once again, the results can be in either direction, for good or for bad. Mobs commit crimes. Society commits crimes in abuse of human rights and other injustices. People also do good guiding emotions away from violence into peace and justice.

### Motivation

A great leader must not only be inspiring and able to communicate his message, but must also be able to motivate specific action. To have a message and be able to deliver it, but to get no results in action is an exercise in futility. It must be a great disappointment to a preacher or a teacher to inspire and communicate but then fail to obtain results.

## Preparation

A great leader must be prepared to lead. A teacher, a doctor, a soldier each requires lengthy preparation to practice his profession. Those are technical professions, in which formal education is an important element. Yet it is possible to be a leader without formal education.

In sports we find leaders who may have only the qualities of preparation and dedication. A baseball player who can hit .300, a pitcher who can win twenty games or a star in basketball, football, golf, boxing, hockey, track or swimming will create a fanatical following. The star athlete's achievements become inspirational to many who desire to emulate him. The fame and fortune that a minority athlete can win are an inspiration to many minority people.

## Dedication

A leader must be dedicated. He must be inculcated with a burning desire to achieve his goal. Without complete dedication, it would be impossible to attain the goal of a great leader. Dedication includes other necessities—determination, consistency and willingness to make great sacrifices towards the attainment of leadership.

## Example

Is it necessary for a man to set a good moral example assuming he possesses the five other qualifications deemed necessary for leadership? We have had great leaders in government, recent ones being Franklin D. Roosevelt, John Kennedy and Winston Churchill. Certainly, it would be difficult to convince many people that these were not great leaders. Yet the morals of the above presumably were not beyond reproach.

I am certain that it is desirable for a leader to set a good example. But would a lack of this disqualify him from leadership? Personally, I think not. I'm certain many will not agree with me.

## Summary

In my opinion, a great leader is inspirational, a good communicator, a motivator, is well prepared, is dedicated and in some instances may be able to set a good moral example. Yet is it necessary to have all of these qualities? Could a great leader have one or a combination of the these? What do you think?

# 15

# EXIT

There is a time for everything. When is the time to realize the necessity for change? I am specifically referring to the actor who has lost his ability to perform in his old style, to the singer who lost his voice and to the athlete who is on the downgrade, having passed his peak. It is so pitiful to see once-greats hanging on to past glories and living a fantasy that although they may have declined a bit, they are still good performers, athletes or what else. The less than acceptable attempts to continue past one's peak are degrading to the once-great contributor to drama, to music or to athletics.

I have seen once-great singers who, because they are unable to recognize their decline, continue fruitless efforts to gratify an insatiable ego for the plaudits of the crowd. This is certainly understandable. It is easier to ascend than to descend, yet time alters circumstances. One justification of this desire to continue can be economic necessity. Many once-famous persons have dissipated their fancy salaries which they no longer are able to command. The compromises then begin. Capitalizing on one's past reputation has a certain marketability in spite of inadequacy in maintaining previous standards.

So down and down they go, accepting lesser and lesser salaries until the pathos begins—the once-great star performs any place for any price, in some instances just room and board.

However, I have known people to perform for food and lodging who really were not destitute and did not need a dole. They are unable to recognize the time has come to change. Their egos live on applause and, in many cases, insincere praise, which is the narcotic for continuity. With better advisors and sometimes more sophisticated new stars, fewer will be faced with economic need after they have passed the peak of their careers.

So far, I have mentioned only the rise and fall of entertainers, the category that contains actors, singers and athletes. But I believe this hanging-on syndrome is applicable to many other professions. I knew of a surgeon, working and teaching in a celebrated medical school. He had enjoyed an illustrious and distinguished career as a surgeon, teacher and writer, but now refused to accept—or perhaps even to recognize—the fact that age had dulled his surgical abilities. He continued to operate until, after a series of unsuccessful operations, he was no longer allowed to operate in the hospital where he had practiced. This man's past excellence cannot excuse the unnecessary problems for his patients. It is sad not to be able to recognize and then accept that the time has come to exit. Age has an effect on us all. Whether or not it slows your thought processes, lowers your stamina, dims your eyesight, slows your muscular response, lessens your hearing or whatever, you are still affected in some ways.

I have never advocated retirement. The wasting of still usable talents is unnecessary and unproductive. As long as a person lives, there are contributions he or she can make to better society. Of course, I am not including people who are senile or severely disabled. Yet, even these people indirectly can be helpful through studies and observations of their behavior which, in turn, may be used to help others with similar afflictions.

What then should the fading star do? Many, many things remain to be done in this world. You will remember that in "Enough," I advocated never retiring or having "enough," but instead to use your surplus, whether it be money, knowledge or experiences, to assist others. I believe the same principles apply here. The actor can teach others and can do social work effectively because of his ability to communicate and dramatize his message effectively. The singer may be able to do the same. The athlete certainly has opportunities available to him as a coach. Literally thousands of jobs are available in all types of schools from universities down to primary schools. Of course, to the professional, a job with the pros as a coach, scout or public relations man may be preferable.

Those suggestions apply to those wishing to stay close to their professions. The aging surgeon can continue his teaching and writing, passing on his experience and knowledge to those more proficient in his past surgical profession. Some talented individuals may leave their past careers and embark on completely new goals, depending upon their age, health and abilities.

There comes a time in everyone's life to prepare younger people to carry the baton in life's relay race. To be able to accomplish the transition gracefully, maintaining one's dignity by not embarrassing past achievements and by continuing to contribute in the best way possible, is achievable. All of those are desirable and necessary before making the final exit.

# 16

# WATER

I am looking out of my window in Miami Beach at the Atlantic Ocean. It is a dull, rainy day. The water is aqua at the shoreline but a deep dark blue, almost a black, in the distance. This is a decided contrast to its colors on a clear sunny day. Usually, a continued gaze at the water can provoke drowsiness. Usually, there is a change in colors from aqua to three or four shades of blue with an occasional strip of green. Usually the peaceful, smooth, calm, sparkling water is very soothing. Today the ocean is angry, limiting its usual rainbow to a few dark ominous colors. Instead of calm, it is turbulent. Instead of being restful and peaceful, it is restless and belligerent.

All of this is another lesson in the close correlation between nature and man. The changing seasons . . . Spring, the awakening, the rejuvenation of the trees and flowers, the planting time for crops. Summer, the maturing of nature through the sun, rain and wind. Fall, the reaping of the work of spring and summer. Winter, the resting, revival, restoring of nature to prepare for the cycle beginning with spring.

Oh, the fickleness of nature, changing its mind without cause or reason. Today, one day later, the fickle ocean has assumed another identity. It is calmer even though the dull rainy day continues. Ripples are on the water instead of angry waves. The color is uniformly pale green with no traces of blue. The hangover of a binge turns the waters to moderation instead of uncontrollable rage. Don't we act like the ocean? I cannot wait for the next episode. Maybe this afternoon? Maybe tomorrow? The next day? We shall see.

It didn't take long. The sun came out. The waters became a satiny sheet. The colors returned. All of them, the aqua, the pale green, the light blue, the dark blue and the medium blue, even yellowish patches were visible, perhaps only in my mind. Temporarily, "God is in His heaven. All is right with the world."

We know the complete tranquility of this incredibly beautiful ocean will not remain. We do not know when or where or if turbulence hasn't already returned. Perhaps not here but elsewhere. We know it will be here in due course. Some fail to enjoy the moment of ecstasy in peace and beauty because they are anticipating the inevitable change to come. Some lull themselves into false security of the permanence of Utopia. Never in this life, on this earth, will anything be permanent. Every second that passes confirms the idea of non-permanence. We move closer to the inevitable departure.

Can't we weather the storm, gather relief from its subsiding and enjoy to the fullest, drinking in every drop of the calmness, the beauty, the peace that results?

# 17

## SPEECH

I was surprised at the large crowd that turned out for the charity black tie banquet. The flattering applause at my introduction as this year's nominee for the guest of honor was ego building. My response was to make the following speech:

"I know it is protocol to say thanks for the recognition given me, so, as I sometimes conform, I will say thanks. However, I would like to apprise you of the facts prompting my reason for accepting this distinction. You know for years I have supported this organization and many others. When I was approached to accept this honor, I was most reluctant. After all, what had I contributed to the organization to be selected? Actually, nothing. Yes, I had given money which I didn't need and which I hope did some good. Does giving something you don't need and without ever making personal efforts to contribute time to attend meetings, serve on committees or help in numerous other ways entitle me to be rewarded? I think not.

"I was told that my acceptance was an opportunity for many people to thank me publicly for what I had done. Since I did nothing, why did they want to thank me? Above all, the only reward I needed I had already received—the inward personal pleasure of feeling good and getting a glow of happiness out of perhaps passing on a small part of that happiness. I also knew that others had turned down the recognition now being received by me. Why then did I accept?

"I am very cognizant of the fact that charities need money. These banquets essentially are fund raisers. The facade of a supposedly well-known person as an honoree will attract people, especially if through business connections and a wide circle of friends and acquaintances he is liked or admired. I was dubious of my crowd drawing ability. I was told a very prestigious committee would guarantee a packed house. From the size of the audience, I see they have succeeded.

"I rationalized all of the above and finally came to the conclusion that since I knew all this was an insincere form of flattery in order to raise money, I was not being duped. However, the results were all that mattered. If the committee believed that I might be part of a conduit to siphon money for a worthwhile cause, which I believed in, why not?"

But, in fact, the above speech is the one I might have made—if I had accepted the invitation to be the honoree.

# 18

# MOLDING

A painter has an idea which he attempts to mold into a picture. A sculptor molds in stone or other media. The singer, actor or athlete molds a performance that an audience will admire. The engineer, architect or builder molds a different object.

The most difficult and rewarding molding is of a human being. The creation was started by God—or by any other force you may care to believe in, such as evolution. The reproduction process of creation was passed on to perpetuate man. This process of molding begins at birth. The baby is nurtured by the parents, who often are the most important influence. Next, the child is turned over to educators, teachers and spiritual molders (preachers). After these introductions to molding, he may be somewhat prepared and aware of the further molding to take place in the continuity of life.

After the preliminary molding, the final and perhaps most important one takes place—becoming molded by life. The world is not necessarily cruel, yet it can be. Adjustment to the fickle quirks of life can be devastating, but it doesn't have to be. Life can be a cake walk, so to speak, but this is not guaranteed. The molding until the end is greatly determined by preparation, environment, opportunity, ability to adjust, strength of character—hopefully molded earlier, desire, pride and you name the others.

To create a great human through molding is, to me, the ultimate—far greater than the works of the painter or the architect of bricks and mortar. This is a molding of flesh and spirit. Let's look at some examples, starting with *My Fair Lady*. Here we find an underprivileged, beautiful woman cast as a cockney flower seller. Her father is a ne'er-do-well. Her companions are drunkards, thieves and other types of shady characters. From this environment, she was plucked by Professor Higgins and molded into a great lady. The outward transformation caused by that molding was matched by the inner growth of character. Do you know any Fair Ladies who have emerged from the depths and reached the heights because of molding? Can you imagine the great thrill of a personal involvement in the molding and the great inner joy obtained from a successful venture?

People are not only molded by other people interested in developing their full potential but religion can be—and often is—a great molder. The rehabilitation shelters, Salvation Army and such, provide food, shelter and perhaps inspiration to many unfortunates. Some few may be rescued and led into a fruitful life through the molding done by these organizations. It is not necessary to be a street person, a thief, a drunkard or dopey in order to need help. Many people develop the "I don't care" or "It's hopeless" attitude and accept a futile life instead of realizing that life can be improved by sensitive, skillful, caring molding.

Many years ago, I knew a hard-working and capable shipping clerk. He had a caring, lovely wife who was a wonderful housekeeper in the tiny rental apartment they could afford. Those were hard times. His only escape and so-called recreation was drinking on weekends. Many a Sunday morning, his wife had to get him out of jail for public drunkenness. He believed his lot was only to eke out a bare existence and his future was hopeless. His boss recognized the potential in this young couple and began the molding process. He suggested they buy a home, offering to pay the down payment. He trebled the man's salary from $25 a week to $75. Dignity, ambition and a sense of humanness emerged in this couple. No more weekend binges but, instead, a love of home. They created a doll house. They emanated happiness and had a purpose, a home of their own. His talents did not permit a job change, but he became even more proficient at his work and a better employee and person. They had been molded into somebodies.

People who have never been presented an opportunity, or who thought they had been bypassed, and complacently accepted this as their destiny, can be fertile fields for successful and rewarding molding. "A diamond in the rough" can be found and developed where least expected.

The rewards to the molder are multiple—the self-satisfaction out of a successful molding and the creation of a new, energetic, happy, good citizen. However, nothing is without its potential pitfalls. Let's take the case of the shipping clerk who had gained a new identity. Suppose something happened to change the euphoria he had developed. $25 a week was the going wage for a shipping clerk, but he was making $75 a week. Suppose the business was sold. Suppose his boss died. What would happen? Chances are the new bosses, purely profit-motivated, would consider him overpaid in relation to the market value of the job. Could he adjust to a pay cut? Could he live with the fact that he had been worth $75 a week but now was offered only $25? He probably would quit and futilely look for the $75 job. What appears to be a great deed might have negative repercussions. Yet, aren't the possible rewards worth the risk? I think so.

In this world, there are many people who deserve an opportunity to be molded into a better outlook, a better life, a change from resignation to welcome the positive challenge of growth and accomplishment. Do you know anyone who qualifies for molding? If so, try it. You may get a great, great thrill out of helping to accomplish the transformation of a person's life.

# 19
## LEAVES

In Memphis, on a chilly, dreary morning in January, with drizzling rain, as I waited for a ride to the office, I looked at the trees all bare of leaves. Even naked, the skinny, sprawling, dark gray limbs portrayed devastated dignity. The strong trunks still proudly carrying their burden without leaves. Of course, in due time the buds will again sprout, the leaves will return, the limbs will be flashing with green.

The leafless tree was like a naked man. Without the clothes or uniform or medals that announce a certain status in life, does the naked body emanate the dignity and strength of the tree trunk? The outward display of wealth, power, honors, may only be camouflaging the insecure body. Can the human, deprived of his outward decoration, adjust and show the strength, integrity and courage of the tree? Even without the cosmetic beauty of its green leaves, the tree is still strong. It sturdily carries on until the beauty returns. The inner beauty has never left.

I find it interesting to watch the charade of people trying to impress and use others by outward, ostentatious behavior—the insincere flattery, the wining and dining bit, the injection of sex, all to accomplish a material end. I wonder what would be the percentage of success in just being honest, sincere and concerned when dealing with people. All the trappings of material success, such as jewels, money, cars, fine homes, yachts, planes and all the other toys of the wealthy have their place.

However, these material possessions are independent of the unworthiness of the possessor. Why can't nature take away and restore just like the tree whose leaves have left, but will return to the trunk that stays strong and maintains its integrity? When this tree dies, other trees, not necessarily relations, will carry on and will maintain the color of leaves.

A perfect example of the thought I am trying to convey is the building of a mansion—a house of startling exterior beauty, fine marble, stone or brick, artistic masonry, beautiful grounds. This is indeed a monument! From the breathtaking beauty of the outside, the interior is very much out of place. Instead of the elegance of the exterior being further enhanced by the interior, the opposite happens. The furnishings are very mediocre, unsuited to the grandeur expected from the outside. All the emphasis and money has been spent on the outside to apparently impress, yet the inside has been completely neglected. Not so with the tree. Not so with some people.

# 20

## SUPER BOWL

Two days from now, January 25, 1987, the 21st Super Bowl will be played in Pasadena, California. I'm sure with all the hype and publicity most everyone knows what the Super Bowl is; however, just in case, it is the World Series of professional football. This is the game for the coveted victor's ring, the recognition and the $36,000 to each winning player. This is the culmination of a strenuous, physical and exciting season of professional football. The teams that won their divisions and their league titles now play against the opposing league for the championship.

Not only in the United States, where an audience of 130 million people is expected to watch television and 13 million to listen on radio, but 38 other countries will receive broadcasts, including Italy's first nationwide coverage. Amazing? I think so. How many people do you think would listen to a concert by all the great living performers? How many would listen to interviews with all the great artists, teachers, preachers, doctors, even politicians? How many companies would pay $600,000 for 30 seconds of advertising time during the game breaks, or $150,000 for 30 seconds during the pre-game two hour program?

What's wrong with all this? In my opinion, *nothing*. This is a once a year climax to a football season that has lasted from spring training for high schools, colleges, universities and professional football teams. This is a sport which develops partisan frenzied support for our teams, whether it be a school we have attended or our children or friends or just because it is in our neighborhood, city or state or, in the case of international competition, our country. Sports are a part of the American heritage. Good, clean, honest, competitive sports develop character, physical fitness, discipline and ability to work with others. Even though over-emphasis on commercialism, dope, gambling and other negatives tend to dampen the predominant positives existing in sports, football and baseball are valuable, and they are essentially American. The Japanese, who like to emulate Americans, have become skillful and most enthusiastic over baseball.

John Madden was a former football player and coach but is now a prominent and excellent television broadcaster in football color and expert analysis. He does not fly and during his numerous train rides, sometimes from coast to coast, passes time by playing "train games." Two of these are very thought provoking. One, if you were stranded on a desert island, what three people would you take with you? My three would be: (1) My wife or female companion. (2) An outdoor friend who knew how to survive with nature. (3) I thought of a doctor, but with no facilities available, how much help would he be? So my third choice would be a good friend, male or female, who was quite self-sufficient, good company and a cheerful helpful participant in the situation.

Another of his "train games" is to rank power, money, love and glory in order of importance. Answers to this will vary according to the circumstances, age, sex and personality of the individual. My rankings are: (1) Love. (2) Money, because with money you can get power and even glory and perhaps a form of love. Of course, money is not the only requisite for power and glory but it is a very potent one. (3) Power. (4) Glory.

What would yours be?

# 21

# LONELY

"You don't know what it means to be lonely," the lady said. "After my husband died, I had everything but companionship. I had plenty of money and good health. I was not too old, I was reasonably attractive, but I was devastatingly lonely. I could not find the type of man I needed for my happiness." But she eventually found a compatible husband and is now quite content.

I have found women to be more lonely than men. Women's lib has eliminated some of the taboos, but women who have been brought up in an earlier era and a more restrained culture cannot accept the idea of going out to dine alone or going to parties without an escort. They are even reluctant to invite a man to a function for which they have tickets. These attitudes make it particularly difficult for many ladies not to be lonely.

The type of woman I am talking about can be a widow, a divorcee or a spinster. She requires male companionship to be happy. Some of these women can adjust to life without a man, yet some cannot and this is the tragic group. To become so dependent on a person is harmful and even sinful. The uncertainties and frailties of life, and the mortality of mankind, make it dangerous to center one's life completely on another mortal. Devotion, love and respect in no way diminish because one mentally is strong enough to proceed in life without the person taken by death or alienated for other reasons.

Unfortunately, many people are not able to adjust to a traumatic change in life. They have been so accustomed to someone doing everything for them—handling finances, making decisions, buying clothes, groceries or anything—that they find themselves helpless when these tasks are no longer being performed for them.

Drastic change inevitably brings stress. And if a feeling of futility and extreme loneliness leads to depression, withdrawal from society and self-pity, how do we cope? Certainly it is easy to prescribe. Certainly, from the beginning of time, similar situations have existed and remedies were suggested and recommended. Let me join the club.

We must recognize the necessity for adjusting. Life is a constant adjustment to the changing conditions. You can do nothing about a death, so you must adjust to it. There is no alternative. You cannot restore the past. Loss of a job is traumatic but not necessarily tragic. Adjust, try to get another job. Maybe it will be better than the last.

Don't crawl into a shell because of adversity. Do everything you can to prevent loneliness. Go out, make friends, change your life. It is essential. Your life has been changed. Accept that fact and do something about it. Get out of the daily regimented routine. Do different things. Any change is a beginning.

Renew a spiritual awakening. Put your trust in a greater power to regain your confidence and ability to adjust to adversity. Fight loneliness!

# 22

# YOU

The most important thing in your life is you. If you accept that, your potential becomes unlimited. But the importance of you does not necessarily imply total disregard for others, arrogance, conceit or any other negative. Certainly you are not an isolated island. You must conform to society's laws and customs, and you must accept life's trials and tribulations. Yet despite those distractions, you must be the most important thing in your life because without you, you are nothing.

Don't limit your growth by the negatives. Don't say to yourself, I am nobody, I haven't any money, I don't have an education or nobody likes me, for in many respects those statements are probably untrue. And even if they all are true, do not despair. No matter what you haven't got, you still possess the greatest thing in your life, you.

Depression, even suicide, can result because of lack of appreciation for yourself. Your imagined ostracism by society because of your looks, color, religion, age or intelligence also is undoubtedly true by the actions of some people—bigots, insensitive idiots who fail to examine and search for the good in the individual. All individuals, no matter what their faults, still have some good. Find it. It is there.

In order for society to reach its greatest potential, every individual must realize how important he really is. There would be no society if people did not believe in themselves. A healthy relationship with society depends upon respect. In a good society each individual is able to discern, accept and appreciate the importance of others. Through the realization of the importance of you, it is possible to recognize the importance others place on themselves.

A society of people who know their own importance, values and self-respect is a giant stride towards Utopia.

# 23
# "?"

Some strange things have occurred in my life. I hesitate calling them miracles, coincidences or fate, so the title will remain a question mark. Consider these four instances:

## Havana, Cuba

In the 1950's, my wife and I were in Miami with two other couples and we decided to spend a weekend in Havana, Cuba. I wanted my brother Louie in Chicago to know I would be gone over the weekend so I phoned him. Louie, who was the buyer of tobacco and whiskey for the Walgreen Drug chain, said he had a very good friend in Havana, Joe Garcia. Joe was from the famous Perfecta Garcia cigar family and sold cigars to Louie. So much for the introductions. I had no idea of calling Joe since we were on only a two-day pleasure trip and wanted to discover things for ourselves.

Friday night, our first night in Havana, we made the round of night spots, had dinner at a fine restaurant and were having a good time—until I broke off a part of my tooth. It was not too painful at that moment because I was partially sedated by the drinks I had consumed. The next morning was different. The exposed root was acting up and I was in pain. That's when we discovered dentists did not work on Saturday. I then thought of Joe Garcia. Arthur Karoff, one of our group, got the telephone book to look for Joe Garcia. Can you guess how many Jose or Joe Garcias were in Havana? Over half a page in the book! I didn't know where he lived; his office, if he had one, was probably closed; and to call all the Joe Garcias in the book would have taken the day. About that time, our telephone rang. Arthur answered and the caller asked if a Mr. Silverman was there. Arthur said no, but that Mr. Moss was. The caller said, "Who? Lou Moss from Chicago?" Arthur said, "No. Morrie Moss from Memphis. Who is this?" The reply: "Joe Garcia!" I got on the phone and Joe said he would get his dentist to see me, even if it was Saturday. He did. I was relieved.

Upon returning to Miami, I told my brother about this lucky incident. It seems Silverman was a caterer at Arlington Park Race Track in Chicago and Garcia sold them cigars, too. Silverman had the same room number as ours but was on the floor above. By mistake, the operator rang my room. Louie called Nate Gross, who wrote a column for the *Chicago American* newspaper headlined, "A Million to One Shot Happens in Havana."

How do you like that one for a beginning?

## Toledo, Spain

In the late 1960's, my wife and I were on a European trip and went to the cathedral in Toledo to see a painting by El Greco. Outside the cathedral were many souvenir stores. In the window of one of the stores was a bell ringer in the shape of a turtle. You could press either his head or tail and a bell would ring. It could be used at a table to call the cook or maid, if you happened to have one. The metal turtle shell was decorated with a pattern of gold threads. My wife liked the turtle bell ringers very much and, as they were not too expensive, she suggested buying several to give our friends. This was a new novelty and would be appreciated. We bought a dozen, gave our address to the shop keeper to ship them and left the store for further sightseeing.

After returning home, we were disappointed not to have received the turtles. Four months passed and still no turtles, so I decided to go right to the top and sent a letter to General Franco about the incident. Imagine my surprise, when a letter came from the Minister of Tourism, who offered every assistance if I could give him more information. I had lost the receipt, didn't remember the name of the store and could only vaguely describe the location as adjacent to the cathedral. Since there were so many stores and since I heard nothing further from the Minister, I assumed he did not have sufficient information to help us. I managed to put the turtles out of mind. Lo and behold, in about two years the turtles arrived without fanfare. No note, no explanation, just twelve turtle bell ringers. We accepted them gladly and made belated gifts. I decided not to delve any further into the mystery of the delivery.

Three months later, we were in Miami when a friend from Mexico City came to visit. He asked whether we ever got the turtles. We were amazed! How did he know about the turtles? It seems Howard and his wife Anita had been on a visit to Toledo. Outside the cathedral they saw a gift shop with turtles and bought one to send us as a gift. After they bought the turtle bell ringer and gave our mailing address, the shop's owner exclaimed, "Moss! That's the name, and Memphis! I owe them a dozen turtles they bought some time ago. We lost their mailing address and they never wrote us so we couldn't send them." Strange?

## London, England

In 1950, winding up a trip to Europe, we were in London with a Memphis couple who had traveled with us. Later that day we would board a train at Victoria Station and travel to Dover where the train would be ferried across the English Channel and then proceed to Paris. We had the day off, so to speak, with no tours or any planned events. The ladies went shopping, so Gilbert and I spent our time in the bar. After several drinks, I got the notion to convert some dollars to pounds. I stuffed the pound notes in my pocket and we returned to the hotel. Our wives, with unconcealed disgust at our inebriated condition, tended to ostracize us. We left the hotel by taxi for Victoria Station to embark for France. Silence pervaded the taxi. When we arrived at the station, Gilbert noticed a bar for men only, which we decided to enter and drink a departing toast to London. Our wives wandered off in the station, probably to look for souvenirs. When we came out of the bar our wives were nowhere in sight. We guessed they would be waiting at the gate for us as we had the passports without which they could not board. Staggering towards the gate, I reached into my pocket and found the pound notes I had purchased earlier in the day. Figuring I had no more use for them, I carefully wadded up one bill at a time and threw them to the side of the walk as we proceeded to the gate. We reached the gate. No wives. Finally they showed up and accompanied us to the train, not speaking a word. I was pushed into our compartment and fell on the berth and went to sleep. In the morning, upon awakening, my wife was not in the compartment. I got up and went to the dining car where the two ladies had sat for the whole night. On the table, our friend Charlene was straightening out pound notes that she took out of her purse, all of which were wadded in a lump. In their walk to the gate in Victoria Station, Charlene had kept stooping and picking up the balls of paper which she had put in her purse. As near as I could figure, every pound I had thrown away, she had picked up. Thousands of passengers go through Victoria Station daily, yet my friend had picked up all the money I had drunkenly thrown away! That's something, isn't it?

## Chicago and Rome

In 1926 the Roman Catholic Eucharistic Congress met in Chicago. At this huge gathering, Catholic clergy and laity from all over the world hold Masses, read papers and discuss religious dogma. The clergy was represented by many cardinals, archbishops, bishops and all the rest of the hierarchy of priests, sisters and brothers. The titular head of the Congress was Cardinal Eugenio Pacelli, the papal emissary. At Soldiers' Field, where the Masses were to be held, refreshment stands were erected to serve drinks and sandwiches. I had just finished my sophomore year at the University of Illinois and needed summer work so applied for a job at one of the refreshment stands. I was referred to a nun, who was in charge of hiring, at St. Rita High School on the south side of Chicago where I lived. She asked me what high school I had attended and then told me that the jobs were for parochial school boys. I told the sister that even though I wasn't Catholic I could sell a lot of hot dogs. She laughed and gave me a job.

The first day of the Eucharistic Congress, a group of about ten cardinals stopped at my stand. My recollection is dim but it seems to me the cardinal leading the entourage ordered a hot dog. They all spoke excellent English, none had any money, but a man who accompanied the group paid for everything. After they ate the hot dogs and left, one of my co-workers asked me if I knew whom I had just served. To my astonishment, it was Cardinal Pacelli, the papal emissary!

Time passes on. In 1939 Cardinal Pacelli was elected Pope and became Pius II and reigned until his death in 1958. In 1950, my wife and I with two friends were in Rome on my first visit to Europe. It was Holy Year, an event held every twenty-five years by the Catholic Church, when pilgrims from all over the world come to pray and receive special indulgences for their devotion. I was in the building materials business at the time and had many Catholic customers whom I knew would be thrilled to get a memento from Rome, blessed by the Pope in Holy Year. Near St. Peter's Cathedral were many shops selling religious objects. My wife and I selected quite a few rosary beads and other curios which we thought our Catholic friends would enjoy and appreciate. I was curious to know how the Pope blessed all these objects. The proprietor of the shop told me that all the merchants took the wares they had sold, and brought them to a special room in the Vatican and laid them in individual piles. Every day, precisely at 4 p.m., the Pope came in and blessed the objects. I asked the shop keeper to take us to see the ceremony. After some persuasion, he agreed. At 3:30 we went to the shop and were escorted across the street to St. Peter's. At 4 p.m. the door opened and the Pope entered with his entourage. He walked right past me as he continued blessing all the packages, after which he left. Imagine a school boy serving refreshments to a Cardinal in Chicago in 1926. Twenty-four years later in St. Peter's Cathedral in Rome, the same Cardinal, now the Pope, passes within touching distance.

# 24

# PREJUDICE

A baseball executive has been fired for making disparaging remarks about blacks. What's new? Why all of a sudden is there such rabid concern for the blacks or for Jews, Italians, Poles, Chinese, Catholics, Protestants, etc.? From time immemorial there has been racism and bigotry. Perhaps, and that is a matter of opinion, it has moderated, even only superficially. Certainly there has been some progress through political power, but outward acceptance does not mean inward acceptance. Prejudices remain ingrained. And religious, ethnic and racial groups are granted a token acceptance. The ecumenical boom is admirable and perhaps is genuinely accepted by a few, but once again is the acceptance only outward, not inward?

What about reverse racism? A congressman has been indicted for an alleged crime. His first outburst is "Racism!" Does the fact that four white people are already in jail and several more whites are under indictment while only one black has been indicted smack of racism?

Segregation in schools is a political football. In fact, is it really true that blacks want to integrate with whites and whites want to integrate with blacks in schools? Equal facilities, teachers and amenities are desirable and necessary. Yet, does compulsory integration solve the problem? Do people camouflage and feign affinity when deep down the prejudices of the past still smolder? Does business acceptance because of economic or political clout modify social customs and prejudices? I believe not. Haven't we still got restricted membership in clubs? Even though an individual may be courted for business reasons, limitations in social equality and acceptance remain.

What is the answer? I know of none. Certainly to say that it's impossible is very negative. Yet realistically, from day one until today, there have always been prejudices, bigots, discriminations and injustice. All these still exist. They have moderated perhaps, but they probably never will be eliminated.

# 25

## MAY 1

May 1 is observed, particularly in communist countries, as a holiday. In 1950, I was in Rome watching the May Day parade marching down one of the main streets. Big banners depicted U.S.A. army tanks and the Soviet Union harvesting in the fields. The connotation was obvious. America was the war monger, Russia the peaceful farmer. Italy had a very large membership in its Communist party. May Day is observed in the United States by labor unions, but not as a manifestation of communism.

Standing in Rome watching this impressive parade of Italians who obviously were true believers in what they were marching for, I was surprised to have a man standing next to me inquire, in excellent English, if I were an American. Of course, I proudly answered affirmatively. He then looked at me with an expression which I characterized as taking pity on me, but later reflection suggested that it wasn't pity but benevolent reproachfulness. "This parade is all your fault," he said. I was startled! What in the world did I have to do with fomenting a workers' parade against war and my country? He proceeded to tell me that the Americans did not understand European mentality. Most Europeans, he explained, had been subject to orders from dictators, kings, clergy and their employers. They were encouraged to follow orders but not to think too much. He continued by saying that America was very generous, pouring money into other countries, but that the giving seemed to end their interest and responsibilities. In other words, here are material things. Go use them to your best advantage. Perhaps not intentionally, the officials distributing the money were not active enough in following up their largess by supervising causes for which the money was being used. As a result, the people were still receptive to persuasion by communist ideas. Here's money. What more do you want from us? Probably more harm than good results from indiscriminate, unmonitored gifts of money.

All of this sunk in and I began to think about wealthy American families. How easy it is for dad, who is busy making money, busy with his clubs, business meetings and travels, and for mama, who has become a social butterfly, to let someone else rear the children. The parents provide the means to have nurses exercise the parental duties of raising their children, and then have the children go to private schools away from home. The parents spend little time with them, and indulge their children's every whim by the rationalization "I want them to have everything I didn't have" or "I had everything when I was growing up and I want my children to have the same." How simple it seems to delegate to others your responsibilities. Is it any wonder that in many cases we find the tragedies of dope, whiskey, a life style fashioned by money, with the parental touch missing?

Recently I heard a particularly poignant story of a poor little rich girl who had been shunted away to boarding schools all her life. One Christmas, she had been asked to stay at the school because her mother and father were going abroad. Yet on Christmas Eve her expectations were aroused when she saw from her window her father's limousine in the driveway of the school. Her father sat in the car while the chauffeur came up to her room with his arms full of gifts. After wishing her a Merry Christmas, the chauffeur returned to the car and drove off. The father hadn't troubled himself to come out and visit with his daughter. The little girl never opened the gifts. She just stayed in her room and cried.

The absence of love in the home invalidates the name "home". Divorces, suicides and all the tragedies of children and parents may be attributed, in most instances, to the lack of love. Wealth is not a substitute for love. I remember the mother of a wealthy, famous man who told me, "Morrie, we are a family of love. If we had only one piece of bread, it would be shared by all of us."

Being rich, poor, middle-class, educated, not educated, religious (although it helps), is not necessarily the criteria. Yet love of your family is the foundation of the happy, healthy family. Acceptance of each member by all the members does not encourage abrogations of one's family rights, duties and privileges. It enhances the beauty. The joy of holidays with families, the exhilaration, the happiness from nearness to family, all emanated by love and conducive to the greatest of happiness, is within the reach and power of us all. Grasp it. Cherish it. Love!

# 26

# MIRROR

We were dining in the Veranda Room on the Queen Mary crossing the Atlantic. A very prominent, wealthy man with his wife and three children were seated at the next table. Perhaps with a touch of envy, I remarked to my group that he certainly was not good looking. The next morning while shaving, I looked into the mirror and at breakfast confessed to my dining companions that I wasn't too pretty either.

The mirror reflects what we look like, not what we think we look like. I had looked at him and imagined that my looks were superior to his . . . until I looked in the mirror. We develop preconceived opinions of how good looking we are or how much we know or how nicely we dress or how well educated we are and perhaps develop a superiority complex. But looking in the mirror can take care of those illusionary misconceptions.

It is easy to close our eyes and imagine grandiose ideas, schemes and desires. When we open our eyes, we awaken to the realization that most of these fancies will not stand the test of light.

Introspection is looking into the mirror of yourself. What are you? We all believe ourselves to have certain qualities, good and bad. Yet, is the mirror reflecting the same thing?

We go to the dentist periodically to keep our teeth healthy. We go to the doctor for check-ups. We go to church for spiritual guidance. Why don't we go to the mirror once in a while and look into what we really are?

# 27

SAD

Radio and now television have made possible the nationwide coverage of politics, sermons, sports and entertainment. In the case of politics and evangelism, the criteria for success depends upon the charisma of the speaker. Good looks and an emotionally persuasive style of speaking can gain public approval and acceptance, while the contents of a speech are secondary.

A strange breed of evangelical religious preachers has captured a tremendous following by their charisma and exposure to enormous television audiences. Their personalities and persuasiveness have reaped untold millions from a worshipful following. The control these people exercise over their audiences is awesome, leading to poverty and disillusion of many followers, and even to mass suicides.

Exploitation through religion is not new. Promises of salvation, indulgences and other spiritual rewards have been available—for a price—to fearful, superstitious or ignorant people for centuries. Today, we are experiencing dramatic upheavals in evangelism for profit. We have seen ministries literally bankrupt because of the extravagant excesses of their preachers. We have witnessed absurd claims and exhortations by many evangelists. Strangely enough, the faithful respond generously to these pleas. Is it a paradox to say you must take to give? The taking of lives in a mass suicide to give absolution of sin is the extreme example.

An accepted adage is "You get what you pay for." Can this be true in the use of religion to extract money from its followers? Is it reasonable to expect the purveyors of the gospel to enrich themselves for their services? Is it conscionable to extract the last dollar from people, even to assignment of their social security pensions, so that the evangelists may bask in the excess luxuries of the world? Even though all religions emphasize helping the poor, sick, aged and helpless, is it wrong to pay money to individuals because of their abilities to generate the funds which, after their share is deducted, the balance may be used for its supposed mission?

Let's go back to "You get what you pay for." How about the person who is lifted spiritually, who is given peace of mind and hope for a better life, and whose despair is changed to optimism? Can you measure his rewards in dollars? He is more than willing to pay money for what he gets.

To be a teacher, a preacher or a purveyor of religious hope is supposed to be a calling from God. The people who respond to this summons are expected to give and to devote their lives to this work, without expectations of material rewards. Isn't it sad that so many people blessed with charismatic persuasive powers can capture a person's mind with the ulterior motive of personal monetary gain? Isn't it likewise sad that people are willing to buy and support these individuals?

Isn't it sad to prostitute religion for personal monetary gain? Isn't it sad to exploit willing people trying to buy salvation?

Think about it!

# 28
# NUTTIN'

"Oh I got plenty o' nuttin', an' nuttin's plenty fo' me. I got no car, got no mule, I got no misery. De folks wid plenty o' plenty got a lock on de door, 'fraid somebody's a goin' to rob 'em while dey's out a makin' more. What for? I got no lock on de door, dat's no way to be. Dey kin steal de rug from de floor, dat's okeh wid me 'cause de things dat I prize like de stars in de skies, all are free. Oh, I got plenty o' nuttin', an' nuttin's plenty fo' me. I got my gal, got my song, got hebben the whole day long. No use complainin'! Got my gal, got my Lawd, got my song."

Wow! Does that pretty well sum it all up? The song from Porgy and Bess, written by George Gershwin in 1935, expresses simple happiness, contentment and security. Porgy tells us what it takes. We don't need to worry about worldly possessions. We all want, need and have probably more than we need. Tragic as the loss of material things and the loss of loved ones might seem, we still can rationalize. We still have other things to prize. "I got no misery." One of life's greatest gifts is good health. I got "de stars in de skies." The whole world is mine! The moon, the sun, the land, the sea, the mountains and the plains. And all are free.

"I got no car, got no mule." That's what I haven't got, but if I had a car and a boat and a plane and a mule and a train and a bus, but had no legs, which would I rather have? I can walk!

"I got my gal." One of the greatest treasures a man can have is his gal—his wife, his family, the happiness of the home created by me and "my gal."

"I got my song." Life is not a series of happy songs. The sad ones appear, yet disappear, and the happy song of the birds, of the wind, of the sea, of the blooming grain and of the heart elevate the spirit of man.

"I got my Lawd." Divine faith, inspiration, benevolence and the peace from the knowledge of a greater, caring power, can eliminate complaining.

Yet, even though Porgy makes a simple, poignant, eloquent statement of the truly meaningful essentials of life, this complicated society which we live in cuts us off from some of the simple desires in his song. Today, a lock on the door may not be sufficient to protect our belongings and provide safety for our loved ones. We probably consider a car is essential transportation in modern existence. And so it goes. Yet, "I got no misery. I got my stars. I got hebben the whole day long. I got my gal. I got my song and I got my Lawd." This leaves little more, if anything, to be wanted. And if this is nuttin', it's good enough for me, too.

# 29

# SPECIAL

Rosie was one of five nursing aides taking care of Lillian, my wife. Rosie must have weighed 400 pounds and her legs often had trouble carrying that massive load without periodical breakdowns. Rosie was very religious. Every year when her Church of God in Christ held its annual convocation, the saints, as members were called, assembled in Memphis for a week of prayer, sermons and singing. The predominantly black membership responded very emotionally to this mass spiritual revival. Loud speakers in the sanctuary raised the sound of the preachers to a roar. The saints responded with loud amens and spiritual renewal. During the convocation, Rosie requested and got a week off to participate.

I forget how many children Rosie had, but they were all special. Rosie worked nights from 8 p.m. until 8 a.m. Her husband brought her to work and picked her up every morning. She was a splendid worker, a gentle giant—kind, patient and efficient. Upon my wife's death, Rosie went elsewhere but kept in contact with birthday cards, Christmas cards and a Father's Day card that particularly impressed me. The card, from Drawing Board Greeting Cards, Inc., Dallas, Texas, was titled:

*Because You're Someone Special*

>Occasionally along life's way, you meet someone you'll always remember. Maybe it's his strength or his humor, the twinkle in his eye or the gentle way he shows he cares, but whatever it is, he becomes very, very special. Maybe he's a helping hand when you need it or a comforting shoulder to lean on or the laughter that puts everything in a better perspective... Maybe he's a source of wisdom, counsel or advice, but whatever he is, he's the one you'd like to have around

when something important is going on (and when nothing important is going on). Life is richer when someone very special is part of it—hope is brighter, faith is stronger, love is deeper, because that special person gives everything more meaning.

Happy Father's Day

And then Rosie wrote, "God bless ya. May ya have menny more happy days. Love you, Rosie."

What a treasure! What a great lift! Indeed, Rosie, you're someone very, very special.

# 30
## CHOICE

Lucy called to borrow $65. They were about to cut her cable television off. Lucy had been an attendant looking after my wife during her long illness. Lucy was probably in her sixties and had a hard time making a living. She had lost her home and tried to get live-in jobs. She had diabetes and could go into a coma at any time. She did not work regularly at our home, but had only filled in when needed. Yet she was dependable, kind and efficient. Like most of the other attendants, she was made part of the family. Shirley, another one of our attendants, had felt herself so much a member of the family that she named her grandson Courtney Marcel Moss.

Lucy was very poor, but had great religious faith and trust. She had borrowed occasionally in the past, but only for vital reasons, such as to pay her overdue utility bill when her power had been turned off in the winter or to pay back rent when she faced eviction from her rented rooms or even, at times, to buy groceries. She always made an effort to repay. At infrequent intervals a money order for $25 would arrive. I felt guilty taking it because she needed it, and I didn't. Yet, would it be demeaning to refuse? I don't know, but after one payment I would usually cancel the debt. My choice was easy.

Lucy had borrowed $50 from me about six months before in the winter to pay her utility bill. She called every month or two to remind me that she had not forgotten her debt and would start paying soon. This morning she called for $65 to prevent her cable television from being disconnected. I asked her if cable was so indispensable to her life. She said her nephew and father like sports and if the cable were cut off they could not follow the baseball games shown daily on cable television. But cutting off cable would not eliminate television reception as the regular non-pay channels were still available. I did some deep, fast thinking. Is this a frivolous, unnecessary luxury? For a poor person how does this compare to the immediate needs of food, shelter and clothing? I remembered the adage that "man does not live by bread alone." Of course, that was spiritual and not applicable to everyday life, or was it applicable? Is a bit of worldly pleasure allowable to people who struggle just to provide themselves with food, shelter and clothing? I had a specific choice to make, $65 or not. While I was rapidly debating this, Lucy added that her father was an invalid, home all the time, and his greatest pleasure came from watching the ball games. What would you have done? I sent the $65.

# 31
# EXPECTATIONS

A great burden is carried by people who feel bound by the expectations of others. A child can feel obligated to comply with the expectation of his parents that he follow a particular career. In school he feels pressure from the expectation to earn superior grades in order to better achieve the planned future. The unfortunate prince must prepare himself for his destiny. His personal ambitions can be stifled by acceding to the wishes of others. Of course, not all cases are alike. Many children may be anxious to emulate a parent or some other idol. They may even relish the opportunity to do what the parent considers necessary to reach the expected goal.

In all the formative years, a life is molded into a plan not conceived by the child and perhaps not even welcomed. With the stress and pressure to maintain these standards, it is perhaps not surprising that some children make futile and counterproductive attempts to escape the pressure by drugs, sex and even deception. I am not saying that these deviations are primarily the result of stress and tension of expectations. Yet that could be a major cause for many victims.

The pressure of expectation extends long past the formative years. No matter the outcome, whether or not the parental desires were ever achieved, whether or not the child chose his own course, there are expectations of society that a person will earn sufficient income to live a comfortable, normal life. Those expectations in turn carry obligations for the government and for private employers. The government is constantly pressured to extend and increase its welfare programs, even though the extent to which many of these governmental programs are desirable and necessary is debatable. The pressure on companies by unions to provide benefits can be counterproductive by impairing the health of the company which, in turn, threatens the stability of the employee.

The most pressure and tension from expectations is experienced by the concerned boss who accepts the responsibilities and problems of his employees. In small businesses where the owner knows most of his employees, a close personal relationship develops, so that the employee's problems become the boss' problems, whether he likes it or not. The poignant plea "I have no one else to go to" transfers the problem to the employer, who is able to alleviate the condition. Like anything else, this can be abused, but isn't it better to have helped when necessary than to isolate yourself from your people's problems because of an occasional abusing of the privilege?

Many times, the continued request for expected assistance becomes irritating and evokes a "Why me?". Yet, why not me? Who else can my people look to? I suppose it might be a relief to know how fortunate I am to be able to help my people.

# 32
# HEROES

The traditional concept of greatness in the monumental people of the Bible, the early explorers, great and powerful rulers, eloquent orators, scientists, teachers, preachers and statesmen, has temporarily been eclipsed by a new hero mania. The great athletes of football, baseball or golf are accepted by many as ideal persons to be revered and even emulated. This adulation goes further in the entertainment field, where a popular singer can be sanctified and his stature grow and perpetuate itself in death. Excesses of alcohol or drugs, homosexuality, womanizing, are accepted as excusable among this very select group and in most cases ignored, if not condoned, by adoring followers.

Although I intend these essays to encompass a broad scope of time, rather than be limited to a current event, maybe the adage that "There's nothing new under the sun" will allow us to see current happenings as a repetition of similar events in the past.

Recently the hysteria for a new idol has emerged in the congressional investigation of illegal covert activities and the bypassing of established legal requirements by certain sincere, passionate and articulate individuals, who rationalized the necessity to violate the law to accomplish a task which, in their opinion, must be done. They think any means towards that end is justifiable.

We watch a charismatic, young, handsome army officer, in full uniform with ribbons of combat and awards emblazoned on his coat, confessing that he lied to Congress and shredded documents that possibly were vital to the investigation. He invokes God, country and patriotic fervor, and explains his actions as simply carrying out orders of superiors and, when necessary, using his own discretionary powers to carry out the mission which, in his view, irrespective of other opinions, is the right and proper course.

The hero-worshiping public places this young man on a pedestal, suggesting he run for the presidency or he should be made

Commander in Chief of the Armed Forces. Haircuts copy his, and foods are named in his honor. Fortunately, this euphoria will not last. Gradually it will disappear and perhaps, when another view is looked at, our hero will fall from his pedestal.

The select panel holding this investigative hearing is composed of members of the Senate and House of Representatives who have been elected by the people to preserve the constitution of the United States and observe its laws. This committee is thought of by our hero not to be trusted with certain information; therefore, he lies to the elected representatives of the people who are attempting to get to the facts for the United States and a world astonished at this fiasco.

I wonder if the members of the committee, who had served their country in the military and in many cases received more prestigious awards, had worn their uniforms with medals, whether the public would have a different opinion as to the quality, loyalty and patriotism of their elected representatives which were being ignored by a hero-worshipping public and charismatic, articulate officer. Portrayed as people not to be trusted with national secrets, even though they were serving their electorate. The public applauding the lies to their representatives. What a paradox!

The laws clearly show the way for a legal covert action. These were illegal, and the laws state the perpetrators of illegal acts are liable, even though acting on orders from a superior. The law forbids certain action which may have been illegal. Yet, temporarily, the mass hysteria has generated the concept of acceptance of the probable violations of their laws.

Time erases much. We will find and idolize and attempt to sanctify new heroes. Would it be too much to expect our next hero to be honest, if not charismatic, to tell the truth instead of proudly admitting he lied? Could our next hero be free from the pitfalls of drugs, alcohol and womanizing? Could our next hero be a person who may or may not have the outward cosmetic facade but the inward spirits of character, honesty, sincerity and loyalty, certainly more desirable qualities than just a pretty face?

Who knows? Hope springs eternal. Yet, we know a golden cow will emerge for our worship. Let's hope for each golden cow we can develop an appreciation and a desire and love for its antithesis.

# 33

# ATTRITION

In 1965, twenty-three years ago, my wife and I invited twenty-eight of our friends for an all-expenses-paid trip to Europe. Their average age was about forty-five, and most of them had never been to Europe. To start this once in a lifetime trip we sent each of them a first-class airplane ticket to New York City, where we spent several days of wining and dining and partying at the Waldorf-Astoria. Then we sailed on the Queen Elizabeth, in first-class staterooms all in a row. At Cherbourg we took the train to Paris, where we spent five days at the luxurious Hotel Crillon and enjoyed the splendid Parisian sights. After that we flew to London for five more days at another fine hotel, Claridge's. London was a great pleasure for antique shopping and visiting many of the historical places. The party officially ended in London with first-class plane tickets issued to all for the return flight to their homes. Some of the group wanted to explore further, so they exchanged their tickets for coach-class tickets and used the refund to pay part of the expense for more European touring.

That's the preamble. Now the story of what changes had occurred after twenty-three years in the lives of those twenty-eight people.

Couple - Wife dead
Individual - Dead
Couple - Divorced
Individual - Married
Individual - Dead
Couple - Husband dead

Couple - Both dead
Couple - Both dead
Individual - Married
Couple - Divorced
Individual - Married
Couple - Divorced and ex-husband dead
Couple - Separated and in the process of divorce. The husband has fathered a child with a live-in companion.
Couple - Unchanged
Couple - Unchanged
Individual - Unchanged
Couple - Unchanged

Of the twenty-eight, only seven were still in the same status as they were during the trip. Eight had died, two were widowed, six had been divorced and one of those had later died, two had separated and three had married. Thus we see the uncertainties of life. The lives of three-quarters of the group have been materially changed through death, divorce, marriage or separation.

Life itself and our relations with others are prone to change. Even the seven people whom I have counted as "unchanged," have had some important changes. Five have retired and the other two are semi-retired. Thus none of the group has retained the same status. Although the trip which brought those twenty-eight people together may have been remarkable, there is nothing unusual about this group. Time brings change to everyone.

# 34

## DEATH

The wife of a very close friend of mine died recently. It is always difficult to find appropriate words of sympathy. Is just "I'm sorry" inadequate? Should I attempt to console him with statements such as "It was God's will," "She is better off dead because of her long sickness," "Her pain is now over," or "She has gone to her well-deserved rest." I don't know. Sometimes the attempt to console can be counterproductive.

A year and eight months ago, I had this ordeal. My wife died. I really didn't need any words of comfort. All I needed was to know and feel that those who had been our friends were still our friends. Words at this time meant nothing. Yet, the desire of friends and acquaintances to express sympathy could not be ignored.

I found the greatest consolation came out of my personal reflections on death. Reams of opinions are available in literature, the Bible and philosophy. What is death? Does the collective perpetuity and the continuity of life suggest that for the individual there is no death, merely a change? People have many beliefs—the indestructibility of the soul, the resurrection of the dead, a heaven, a Messiah, a reincarnation, the return in a different form. Is an afterlife a reality? Do we meet again in heaven, reuniting with loved ones or even resume a stormy relationship completely altered in the afterlife? These beliefs can be comforting.

Certainly it is true that "Time heals all wounds." But how does it heal? Probably by the adjustment to the fact that the hurt has occurred and cannot be reversed. Therefore, time dulls the emotions of the moment and tempers the feeling by resignation and acceptance of the realistic present.

How do we respond to a death? Do we think it an interlude and a change that will be remedied, corrected and resumed at our own death? Or do we think of it as the end of an era—a completed, finished episode of our life and, that being over, we start anew with another phase of our life? Adopt whichever seems to be more comforting to you. Maybe a third alternative, which combines the first two, will be more viable: This is only a transitory period, but in that interlude I will continue my life's path with new adventures until I return in death to the old ones. Problem: Supposing the new era is more desirable than its predecessor?

# 35

## AMAZING

A good friend went into the Doughnut Shop and ordered seven dozen doughnuts—seven packages of one dozen each—three glazed, three chocolate covered, three cherry filled and three crullers or French doughnuts. The salesperson remarked, "This is a very large order and it would facilitate our baking schedule if you would call us a day ahead, and it would also save you time as they would be packaged on your arrival." This was agreeable to my friend. The clerk asked what he was going to do with all these doughnuts. My friend said he was going to give them away to some of his friends. The clerk asked what was the occasion for the gift. My friend replied there was no occasion. The clerk responded, "Amazing!" I guess it could be characterized as unusual, but amazing?

It is customary to give gifts, cards or a recognition of some sort to celebrate important happenings, such as a wedding, an anniversary, a birthday, Christmas, confirmation, engagement, even a funeral. This is not considered amazing but purely protocol. Why shouldn't one, as the telephone company suggests, "reach out and touch someone" whenever the urge presents itself or just when thinking of a friend or acquaintance. The conversation needn't be lengthy or inquisitive. Just say, "I was thinking of you today and simply wanted to hear your voice, which always brings back pleasant memories." Then you can enjoy the appreciative, surprised response which opens up a rewarding, refreshing renewal of a friendship. Talking is not the only way to show interest and concern about a friend. Write a note, send a card, not because it's a special occasion (every day is special) but because you really care.

The impromptu urge to contact someone just because you

wanted to call, send a letter, a card or even a doughnut, gives you satisfaction. But the recipient's pleasure is greater because of the spontaneity of the contact. The monotony of a routine existence is pepped up by unexpected pleasant surprises.

# 36

# APPRECIATION

I was shopping in the supermarket when an old man came up to me asking if I was going to buy $15 worth of groceries. I replied that probably I would. He then wanted to know if I was going to buy the special of the week which was a pound of coffee for 89 cents with a coupon and purchase of $15 or more in groceries. Since this was not our brand of coffee and since we did not need any, I answered him no. He asked if I would use his coupon to buy it for him because he didn't have $15 to buy the additional groceries necessary for the bargain special. Yes, I would. Upon completing my shopping and checking out, the man was waiting for me outside of the checking stand. I gave him his coffee. He offered to pay. I declined the payment, but had a hearty laugh when, instead of thanking me, he asked, "Where are the stamps?" Some stores give bonus stamps, in amounts determined by your purchases, that are redeemable for merchandise. I do not like to think of this man as unappreciative. In his mind, I received some stamps because of his coffee purchase so, even though he hadn't paid for it, he probably rationalized if he had not requested the coffee I would not have had those stamps. This mind reading, of course, is merely an effort to condone an obvious lack of appreciation.

Another lack of appreciation may be construed by positive vocal thanks, yet negated by mental reservations. It was nice getting this raise, bonus, present or whatever. But then, why shouldn't I get it? I need it more than he does; he's got plenty; I deserved more than I got; this is just a long due recognition of what I should have gotten some time ago. No matter what the rationalization produces, isn't it true that somebody gave, somebody took? Would unreserved appreciation be inappropriate?

Someone does a big favor for someone else—and puts himself

out to do it. Then he is perfunctorily thanked because the recipient, instead of feeling unreserved appreciation, thinks "Why shouldn't he? I would have done the same for him under similar circumstances."

It seems difficult to express true appreciation without strings attached. Subjectively or overtly, the motives or reasons for the deed seem to require inward analysis to justify being appreciative.

# 37

# BEAUTY

What is beauty? Is it the glamorous, good-looking individual? Is it nature, the sky, the earth, the sea? Is it literature, great poetry, prose, biography? Is it painting, sculpture, architecture? Is it learning? So, on and on, we could ask what is beauty?

Since beauty is said to be in the eyes of the beholder and eyes have a way of seeing things differently, I would like to suggest that perhaps there is beauty in everything.

Let's go over the questions in the first paragraph, one by one. An individual possessing physical traits of beauty: In this case, assuming the pleasing look to be beautiful, wouldn't the inside of the person be a better criteria of true beauty, rather than the facade? How often have we heard, he is beautiful inside? In this case, we broaden our scope of beauty from the visible to the spiritual or invisible qualities which, though they can't be seen directly, can be observed by deeds.

Who can question the great beauty of nature? The sky with its majestic clouds, soothing rain, thunderbolts of sound and a rainbow's spectrum of color. The earth with its changing seasons, its warmth and its cold, its fertility and its barrenness. The vast seas comprising the greater part of the earth, with all of their individualistic characteristics. Yet, once again, isn't all of this visible? What about the creator of all this panorama of beauty and not-so-beautiful? Is He visible through His creations or is His visibility purely spiritual, with the earth just one of His wonders? Then too, when we say creator, what are we referring to? A deity, an evolutionary development or nature or what?

Books contain much beautiful writing. The great books of the past live on and on because of their message. Some poetry has sensual beauty and is a search for truth through beauty. As Keats asserts, "Beauty is truth and truth is beauty." The spiritual beauty of the Bible, the inspirational qualities of the great leaders of history as retold in records of their achievements and deeds. Certainly these things are a part of beauty. Great appreciation for the visual arts creates a conception of beauty. The transformation of canvas, marble or brick into a painting, sculpture or building becomes a visible pleasure.

Since you can never get enough learning, so perhaps can you never get enough beauty.

# 38

# COLOR

I was looking at a diamond ring in a prestigious Palm Beach jewelry store. The diamonds sparkled under the store's lights. Even my ring took on a new brilliance and I wondered if the artificial lights in the store magnified the beauty and fire of the diamond. When I expressed my concern that perhaps the store's lighting was responsible for a new-found color, the jeweler replied, "Let's go out into God's light and see." God's light—the true light. The sun was shining brightly, and the sparkle, brilliance and color of the diamond were surprisingly better and more magnificent. No doubt about it. This was it. God's light.

This is the fall of the year and the grand finale to another cycle in the year and in life. The fall will end and the new year will host winter, the returning spring, the summer and once again the fall. It seems that as a farewell to the last season of the year nature stages a gala extravaganza, a dying year but exiting in a blaze of color. The crisp fall mornings seem to encourage the sky to flash its spectrum of blues. The cool pleasant evenings bring out a full harvest moon, so big, so round, so bright, so beautiful as to suggest the lighting up for nature's last ball of the year. The day brings God's light, illuminating the beauty of the changing color of dying nature—the scarlets, the browns, the golds, all glistening in God's sunlight as if the beautiful dresses at a ball were copying the colors.

This is a time of dying, yet maintaining dignity and donning a shroud of color. We know the leaves will fall, the colors will fade and life will end or just rest waiting for the resurrection of spring. Yet, like the beautiful flowers on a casket, these will wither and die like the corpse within the casket. All of this taking place in God's light.

# 39

# DISSENT

The right to dissent is one of the greatest privileges of democracy. To be able to stand up and express your disagreement with anything is a right not to be abused. However, dissent and change are two different things. Change involves risk, the acceptance of the unknown and a reluctance of other people to change. In a democracy, change can be accomplished legally by the ballot. But, on the other hand, American corporate structure is a totalitarian. The boss can be wrong, but he is still the boss. Dissent is not possible singly because of lack of power. Collectively, a union can dissent for many people and in some cases enforce change.

Religion is not a democracy. That is why there are over 300 branches of Christianity. These were created through dissent with no option for change—hence the only way to get the change was to start a new church. Is it wrong not to change? I think not. An old cliche applies here: "If it's not broken, don't fix it." The traditional Catholic church has existed for 2,000 years. The orthodox Jewish religion has existed over 5,000 years. Fundamentalist Protestant sects have existed a long time. The many other religions all have long and successful lives. Yet we may hear, you can't stop change; you must keep up with the times; new needs of the communicants must be addressed. But are those changes essential? Religions are the bulwark, the sustenance, the hope of a majority of people. Their strength comes from stability, from the realization that their beliefs are based upon an unswerving faith and devotion. Change would destroy these things. The church, synagogue or mosque cannot change its dogma to accommodate a particular fad or new style or a minority desire. To change would destroy the illusion of the perpetuity of an unchangeable belief. Therefore, in order to preserve the functioning of an institution to minister to the spiritual requirements of the great masses, stability (not flexibility) and permanence (not change) must of necessity be maintained.

I find myself marveling at my words, because it is the exact antithesis of what I believe. As a liberal, change is essential and important. Yet, I do not see myself as a hypocrite because my sincere belief is that change is not a requisite for many. In fact, it would be counterproductive for most. In order to have a religion attractive to most, it must observe its tenets without deviation. If a religion says its priests must be celibate, they must be. If another religion says women cannot be rabbis, then they can't, in the orthodox faith. The tradition should remain inviolate. Accommodations are made in other religions for dissent or different goals. If dissent erupts, it is the dissenter who must change, not the institution.

In monarchies, dissent can usually only result in change through a military rebellion. In democracies, minority groups daily engage in peaceful rebellion to seek recognition. Those groups try to accomplish change by persuasion, but at times can become militant through riots, with accompanying pillage and arson.

I conclude that dissent is a necessary ingredient of a free society. Yet dissent without change is futile. Some things won't and shouldn't change. You do not continue the dissent, you adjust to acceptance or you change.

# 40

# SORRY

I'm sorry! The victim of the drunken driver is a paraplegic, crippled for life. Yet the perpetrator of this tragedy is sorry. "The road to hell is paved with good intentions." "The evil that men do lives after them." What good is sorry to the victim? Is one absolved from guilt because of a confession? Of course, the obvious answer to sorry would be don't do anything to be sorry about. This seems to be impossible.

Yet sorry doesn't always involve the giver. An expression of sorrow for others may or may not be comforting. Bereavement, sickness, accidents, all may require an expression. Sorry may be acceptable.

Another connotation of sorry would be derogatory appraisal. This is a sorry group of students, athletes, people. This is a sorry lot of produce, textiles, manufactured products. In this context, sorry becomes an adjective describing so-called inferiority.

Does sorry imply never doing the thing that you are sorry about again? No! Many people, though believing themselves absolved by expressing sorrow and motivated at the time to never do the sorrowful act again, do it again. A liar, a philanderer, a thief, a dope addict, a drunk who does not have the character to reform.

It is hypocrisy to expect perfection from imperfect persons. Theologically, it is presumed that no mortals are perfect. Yet we castigate, criticize, penalize and in many cases ostracize people who have erred. It is generous, compassionate and only right to forgive trespassers of convention and of the law, after they have confessed, repented, and paid the penalty. Yet, this is not the case. We find a candidate for the Supreme Court withdrawing his candidacy because it was revealed he had used marijuana several times. It wasn't done recently. It wasn't addictive. It was accepted in the society he was a part of. Yet sorry was not enough. At the same time, forgiveness does not apply approval of a law transgressor being in a position where he will judge other similar transgressors. How can he justify punishing law offenders for the same crime he admitted but was not prosecuted for?

In my essay 14, "Leadership," I expressed my opinion that a good moral example is not necessary, although preferable, for a great leader. I have used as my examples great leaders whose lives have not been particularly moral. Some of these men were just following the customs of the times. Some of our great colonial leaders, founders of our country, were slave owners. This terrible blight on human dignity was apparently acceptable to the majority of people. It would be ideal, even Utopian, to have leaders as pure as Caesar's wife was supposed to be—yet is it possible? Is it realistic? I say it isn't!

We have the scourge of drugs, perhaps the most deadly of today's problems. Yet we find that drugs are acceptable to millions and indulged in by many. It is socially acceptable and perhaps a requisite in certain societies. We find several presidential candidates admitting, repenting and quitting drugs. Yet, in a society where drugs are illegal, can we elect a president who has indulged in drugs? Yes we can!

Errors of youth and inexperience are easier to condone than those of adults. In a permissive society, many old hidden customs—homosexuality, women smoking, drinking in public, use of dope, marijuana (smoked for ages by many societies), flaunted promiscuity—have been accepted by many. Acceptance, of course, does not make them right. Going in circles, what is right? Who determines it?

We can rationalize that the private life of a judge, a candidate for public office or anybody in the public eye (whether a preacher, teacher, actor or a sports personality) is not the public's business. In a way, that is correct. Yet, if the personal life of one influences the life of another, or many, shouldn't that be a concern to all?

How do parents respond to a child caught using drugs when he says, "I'm only doing what the President did when he was my age." So, even when we forgive as youthful indiscretion, nevertheless the potential for future damage might exist.

Since no one is judged perfect and since people are needed for judges, presidents, preachers, teachers and all the rest in a position to influence behavior in others, what do we do?

# 41

# LANDMARKS

The newspaper reported this morning in December 1987 the coming demise of three downtown Miami landmark buildings. Two were formerly prestigious hotels. One opened in 1920, the other in 1926. These are being torn down to be replaced by more of the towering skyscrapers that now isolate and surround them. The third building also was a hotel started in the 'Twenties. It was destroyed in 1926 by a hurricane, rebuilt and opened in 1951 as a hotel school by the City Board of Education, the only hotel in the world operated by a city school system. Thousands of students attended over the years, learning trades as diverse as airline stewardess to millinery and watch repair. Maintenance of the building became too expensive. Its eulogy will be: "It's served its purpose." By June 1, 1988 it will be a parking lot. Amen.

Bill has worked well for 35 years. He, too, has served his purpose. Give him his watch, his social security and a small pension, and then say goodbye. Poor Bill. What does he do? He is not a building that can be torn down and replaced. He is a human whose life style has been drastically changed.

Fortunately, there is now a realization of the value of the individual, and laws have been passed to prohibit forced retirement for capable, healthy, aged employees. Whereas this is good for the employed, it becomes discouraging for the younger employee looking to replace the older one. Promotion can be deferred to the point where the younger employee leaves for more opportunistic fields. In turn, this affects the company by not having capable, experienced apprentices to fill the jobs vacated by the elderly.

So, if you are an employer, you have compromises and decisions to make about retirements. You are not dealing with brick and mortar—your subject is flesh and blood. And every situation is different. The personalities involved, both young and old, will not be the same, and no cure-all formulas are available. Some elderly will relish retirement. Some young will have enough patience to wait.

It is difficult for employers to blend the old and the young in an equitable, compassionate manner. This is indeed a Herculean assignment. But the innovative will address and resolve the problem.

# 42

# TURMOIL

Sunday, February 28, 1988, the papers reeked with troubles. Was Armageddon really on its way? *The New York Times* front page headlines announced: "Leaders Agree to Suspend Armenian Unrest," "For Families of Hostages Ire and Hope," "Tension in Electronic Church Illuminated by Swaggart Fall," "Little Gain Seen as Schultz Visits Jordan and Syria," "Panama President Flees from Home" and "Reaping Loneliness on Midwest Farms." The only good news on the front page was: "Florida Weather Sunny and Mild." *Page 3:* "Rightist Rally in Pretoria, Urging a White State" and "Commander of Indonesia Armed Forces Replaced." The good news? A 1751 silver coffee pot at Tiffany's for $9,500. *Page 4:* Ads and "NATO Unity is Called Problem for next President." *Page 5:* Ads and "A Risk of Unrest Seen in East Bloc." *Page 6:* "India Lawyers Handcuffing Spurs Bitter Fight at Courts," "13 Philippine Soldiers Killed" and "Moscow Opens Its Door a Bit to Former Citizens." *Page 7:* Ads. *Page 8:* "The White House Grapples with a Problem of Inconsistency." *Page 9:* "U.S. Charges Cuba Smears Delegate." *Page 10:* "Fatal Siberia Jet Crash is Reported by Moscow." *Page 11:* Ads. *Page 12:* "Another Day of Bloodshed in Occupied West Bank," "Violence Brought Dead to 71," "Iraqi Planes Attack Teheran Refineries" and "Virus Discoveries in African Outpost on AIDS Research." *Page 13:* "Rioting in '87 Gathering in Mecca Prompts Review of Security Procedures," "Change in Manila: Pen or Sword" and "Canada Has Difficulty Deporting Palestinian Convict." *Page 14:* "Protest Group Disrupts a Klan Rally in Dallas," "Northwest Airline Strike Postponed" and "Union Seeking Affordable Day Care at Harvard."

*Page 15:* "U. S. Indicts 4 in Payola Case," "U. S. Warns Aspirin Makers," "Philadelphia Trash Boat Returns" and "Light Infantry Given a Taste of the Real Thing." *Page 16:* "4 Sentenced in Prison Escape," "Swaggert Effort at Deal" and "New Jersey Asserts Right to Tidal Land." *Page 17:* "Battle for Black Vote Over Before It Started" and "Infighting by 6 Democrats." *Page 18:* "Attack on Black Woman Stuns White New Jersey Town," "Connecticut Weighs Insurance Curbs" and "U. S. Agency Ends Exemption for Young School Bus Drivers." *Page 19:* "New York Police Search for Killers," "Drug Rivalry Key to Slaying," "2 Rob Jewelry Store of 4 Million in Gold," "Informer is Defense Witness" and "Minister Suggests Maddox as Brawley Prosecutor." *Page 20:* "Death Notices." Then, after four pages of sports, the first section ends. Have you had enough? What have we read? War, rape, AIDS, murder, theft and sex. Almost all negative. Hardly anything positive. Has the world gone mad? Where is the sanity?

The prestigious *New York Times* proudly announces its motto, at the top of the front page: "All the news that's fit to print." Evidently the *Times* does not consider good news (and certainly there must be some) worthy of first-section coverage. Are all these problems new? They probably are not. But modern communications have brought them wider distribution than ever before. More people are aware of the news of the day, wherever and whenever it occurs. In spite of all the bad news that is so vividly publicized, old-fashioned goodness remains very prevalent. Perhaps people are not as interested in learning about the normal hard-working, God-fearing, good citizens—the teachers in our schools, doctors, preachers, philanthropists, honest office-holders. The preponderance of people are decent and normal. Probably their activities will not sell newspapers.

# 43

# PRESTIGIOUS

"You have been selected to be honored with the year's most prestigious award." I was told this by a member of the selection committee for an annual "brotherhood banquet" to recognize one Catholic, one Protestant and one Jew who supposedly represent the ecumenical spirit of those three religions.

Two things troubled me. One, that this was announced as the "most prestigious" award. Two, the sincerity of brotherhood.

Prestige (most, less, whatever) is certainly not accepted by all people the same way. To me, the brotherhood award was far from the most prestigious recognition. Prestige, like beauty, is in the eye of the observer.

I was reminded of an incident that happened about thirty-five years ago. An out-of-town friend, passing through, stopped for a visit. When I asked him where he was going, he took out a strand of large, lustrous pearls and said he was going to Texas to visit a wealthy woman whom he hoped would buy the pearls for $275,000. I was staggered by the price and I was ignorant of the quality or value of pearls. I blurted out, "Who will know these are real and of such great value?" The response was "She will!"

You yourself will know how much prestige an award carries, and will not depend on what someone tells you. What is a prestigious award? Well, to stand in front of 1,000 people in black-tie evening dress, and listen to generalities and Utopian ideas that are still to be accomplished, may be prestigious to some. Not to me.

There are persons who, while shunning publicity, are dedicated to looking after institutionalized old people or who inaugurate programs for sufferers of Alzheimer's disease and other incurable illnesses. Other, equally unrecognized persons, support children's hospitals and medical research centers or individually help mentally ill children or adults. Anonymous supporters provide financial contributions or work voluntarily for education, the arts and many forms of civic responsibility. All of those people are prestigious contributors. Who knows about them? Who recognizes them with prestigious awards? The persons themselves know. Therefore, they have the most prestigious award.

The second point that troubled me, sincerity in brotherhood, reflects the concerns I have tried to address in my essay 24, "Prejudice." Under the euphoric atmosphere of brotherhood, the words can flow from the honorees espousing their ecumenical beliefs. How sincere are these? The words come from the mouth. What about from the heart? Do the people believe completely in what they are saying? The hypocrisy is obvious. Tomorrow they will be a black, a Jew, a Catholic, a Protestant. A brother? Probably never.

# 44

# THE IMPORTANCE OF UNIMPORTANCE!

What is important? Oversimplification would suggest we are born and we die. Yet, in between, other events which we call important occur. We grow up, we go to school, we marry, we have children, we have grandchildren. This sequence brings other dates of importance—confirmation, graduation, birthdays and anniversaries. Some will say, "You haven't even mentioned the most important thing in life—which is work, doing a job, making a living, taking care of your family and yourself." The gradation of these depends upon the individual. Irrespective of grade, all are important.

Holidays such as Christmas, Thanksgiving, Labor Day and Fourth of July are important, not just for their significance but also because they are occasions for families to assemble in festive, loving and happy reunions. This is particularly true when members of the family who live in distant places return for the celebration.

Those occasions occur infrequently, but what about the rest of our lives? What is unimportant in living? If we accept the premise that life is worthwhile, then every second of the short existence on this earth is important as an integral part of a worthwhile life.

Most of our lives are spent in activities that may be considered unimportant. We get up in the morning, we bathe, we dress, we eat breakfast. Some go to work, some to school, some stay home, some do nothing. We may complain the repetitive monontony of sameness is boring. Probably so. We may complain our work prevents us from enjoying the trees, the flowers, the sun or our friends. Yet, irrespective of desires, our work consumes so much of the time in our lives, it could be considered the most important.

I have had trouble accepting the conclusion that time is the principal determining factor of importance. Logically, if every second spent in this life is important, the activity that engages most of our time would be the most important. But finally, I have reached this personal conclusion: Time is not the only component in determining importance. The degree of importance for any activity is determined by each individual. What is important to one person may be unimportant to another. For example, marriage could be unimportant to a bachelor. Yet he would consider the marriage of his parents important. Even though every second of life becomes important, there is no uniformity of life in individuals; therefore, importance must be determined by each life according to the activities of that life.

I would suggest every moment of our lives is important. The degree of importance is determined by our own personal evaluation. In living a full, productive life which leads to happiness, we realize that everything happening to us is a part of our life and, therefore, since our life is important, any part of that life is important. Nothing is truly unimportant, although its degree of importance depends upon the individual.